The Art of Compromise
Aural Piano Tuning

By James Musselwhite

The Art of Compromise
Aural Piano Tuning

Library of Congress Cataloguing in Publication Data

Synopsis:
An introduction to the Art of Piano Tuning by ear.
Musselwhite, James E.
The Art of Compromise
1. How-To – Guides, Information, etc.
2. Music - Piano, Piano Technicians, Piano Technical,
etc.
I. Title.

ISBN-13: 978-1468150742
ISBN-10: 146815074X

Second Edition © 2018 James Musselwhite

My thanks to the following teachers:

Robert Lowrey

Dick Lewis

Gordon Fishwick

George Diefenbaugh

Mrs. Robinson

David Ferguson

Hugo Spilker

Grant Smalley

Nikolai Svinarenko

Earl Ewing

John Musselwhite

All My Clients

and...

my Father.

Table of Contents

Preface

This is a little handbook for those wanting to learn how to tune, or wanting to improve their tuning skills. Before you pick up this book, you should ask yourself four simple questions:

1. Is this something I am or could be passionate about?

2. Do I love music, and music making?

3. Am I the type of person who likes to work independently, yet enjoys dealing with people?

4. Do I have the patience and time to commit to learning a challenging skill?

If you answered yes to the majority of these questions, and are mechanically inclined with good problem-solving skills, then I encourage you to press ahead.

Piano tuning is a handy and interesting skill to have. You can use it to make pocket money, or a full-time income. However, to be a bad piano tuner is a sacrilege. As professionals we strive to not only be good at what we do, but educate the public as well. To tune a piano poorly in order to make "a quick buck" is not only cheating the customer out of their money, but also robbing them of the experience of having a properly tuned instrument. This can cause students to lose interest, owners to lose trust, and fellow tuners to lose respect.

To be a professional piano tuner, you must strive to be as skilled, honest, and informative as possible.

Even if you are just starting out, I would encourage you to join the Piano Technicians Guild. Not only is it a top-notch source of education and support, but the PTG also tests and accredits new tuners. Associating yourself with the PTG will ensure that you can reach your goal. Having the support, encouragement, and help of fellow tuners is the only way to make sure that you are upholding the highest standards in this field.

James (Jamie) Musselwhite.

Foreword

Tuning a piano is a skill, a craft and an art. Knowing how to tune, tuning, and understanding tuning are three completely separate things. My father patiently demonstrated to me how to tune, but it took a long time to learn how to do it myself. It took an even longer time to really understand, and be comfortable with it.

There are many skills that have to be learned to tune a piano accurately, but there are just three basic parts to each tuning. The first, and the most important from a tuner's point of view, is called "Setting the temperament". This is the foundation on which the rest of the tuning is built, and the hardest part to master. It is also rather difficult to explain.

The musical scale that Western ears have become accustomed to, and upon which the tuning of a piano is based, consists of twelve notes: C, C#, D, D#, E, F, F#, G, G#, A, A#, and B. This arrangement had been invented and used long before any of the composers we know of had been born. So, when they did get here, they inherited a system of music that they were forced to use, even though it has a few nasty little problems.

The main problem has its root in something called harmonics. If you play a string, and then divide it in half by placing your finger on the middle of the string (what physicists call "the node"), you would hear a note one octave higher than the first note, which is called the "Fundamental". (If you play middle C on a piano, and the C above it that is in tune, that is an octave.) If you then divide that half in half again, you would hear a 'Perfect Fifth' above the octave. (Like playing C and the G above it.) If you continued to subdivide the string in this manner, you would hear a rather mysterious thing: a note two octaves higher, then a third (C to E) above that. Then the fifth, then a minor 7th (C to A#), then all the diatonic notes (like all the white keys), and then every single note. If you could go even further you would hear microtones, which are not part of the western scale, but which are a part of the music of other cultures.

This is all fine and dandy, except for a problem known as the "Pythagorean Comma". The first interval of a perfect fifth in harmonics is "pure"; that is to say, it does not have any warble or vibrato, called "beats", when the two notes, the fundamental and the fifth, are played together. All the intervals after this are also "pure" with the note previous to it, but they grow increasingly sharp of the fundamental to the point that the octaves are not "pure" with each other. They become sharp because of the "Comma", which is a microtone that is missing in our western scale. So, in effect, we actually squeeze what is harmonically thirteen notes into our twelve-note scale. This is called "tempering" the scale, and the way in which we squeeze it is called the "temperament".

When there were no keyboard instruments, this was not a big problem. Instrumentalists and singers learned to tune each note as they played or sang, so that they would be pure to any other notes played or sung with them. Since pianos and other keyboard instruments cannot be re-tuned on the fly, dealing with this became a problem that no one has really been able to solve completely.

Before J.S. Bach's time, harpsichordists dealt with the problem of temperament by constantly tuning. They would play a piece in say, E flat, and then re-tune the instrument to play in a different key, like A or D. Large pipe organs of the time would have different temperaments in separate sets of pipes, called "ranks". To play in a different key, you would change ranks. This method of changing temperaments was not only awkward, but still resulted in some intervals sounding horribly out of tune.

The problem was eventually solved, or at least re-solved, during Bach's lifetime. A number of people figured out how to temper the scale in a relatively equal manner so that whatever key you chose to play in, it would be relatively in tune. To demonstrate this new method of tuning, Bach wrote two preludes and fugues for every key, and called the collection "Das Wohltemperierte Klavier", "The Well Tempered Keyboard". Well tempering was the first step towards the acceptance of equal tempering, in which every interval was tuned equally "well". Many musicians at that time disliked the relative out-of-tune-ness of every key that results in equal tempering, so it took a period of time for them to "evolve" into accepting it. The "Equal temperament" is now the standard tuning in every modern keyboard instrument.

The temperament, set into an octave in the middle of the keyboard, is the first thing that is done when a piano is tuned. After that, one string of every set of strings per note is tuned from the temperament octave. When I say "set", I am referring to the fact that in the mid-range and treble (top) of the piano there are three strings per note, in the tenor there are two, and in the bass there is just one. Finally, the other strings in the sets of strings, called "unisons", are tuned.

When I first started to tune, my Dad would do the first two steps, and then I would do the last. As I mastered this, he would move me onto the previous step. Each step is an art in itself, and it takes a lot of practice to do it well. There is also the matter of learning to become comfortable with the tuning tool, called a "hammer", not to mention the differences between pianos.

When a piano is tuned properly, it is actually put very accurately out-of-tune, because each interval is slightly compromised. It is no wonder, therefore, that my Dad used to call his trade, "The *Art* of Compromise".

Lt. Col. F.W. Musselwhite III
The author's grandfather,
with his tuning kit, circa 1930.

The Mechanics of Piano Tuning

To make money as a tuner, all the tools you really need could fit into your back pocket. This is one of the main advantages to learning how to tune a piano by ear. I can, and have, driven into a town in the middle of a longer journey, and within a few hours, made enough money for a meal and a hotel room. I didn't need a heavy tool kit, or a laptop computer or some other machine. All I needed was my ears, my skills, and the confidence to sell my services.

Of course, to repair or regulate takes a much larger tool kit, and a good deal more skills, but to just tune, all you need is a hammer, a tuning fork, a rubber mute, a Papp's mute, and a temperament strip.

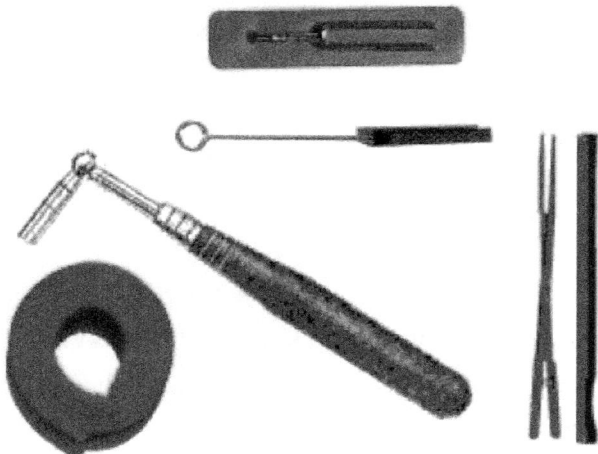

The Tuning Hammer

You need a professional quality tool to do a professional job. The tuning hammer normally stocked in your local music store is what is called in the trade, a student, or chipping hammer. Significantly cheaper than a professional hammer, it is lightweight, fixed in length, and does not have a removable tip. A professional hammer, available from a piano supply company, is heavier, balanced, can extend in length, and not only the tip, but the entire head can be removed. The handle is either made from nylon (as shown) or hardwood. Both the head and the tip come in different lengths.

The shorter the tip, the more the torque is transferred into the axis of the pin rather than the length. However, on some pianos, a short tip may not allow the handle to pass over the lid on upright pianos, or the plate struts on grands. The head can also come in different angles so that when the hammer is on the pin the handle rises either perpendicular to the piano or in varying degrees away from the piano. It is also important to be able to change the tip after it has worn too much to grab the pin adequately. The handle can extend, increasing leverage, making pins that are too tight in the block easier to turn.

Generally, the hammer is held at the very end when moving a pin; however, there are times when small adjustments can be made more accurately by grasping the handle closer to the head. When placing the hammer on the pin on an upright, align the handle so that it is more or less straight up and down. Grasp the end of the handle firmly, and hold your forearm so that it is level with the floor. Large movements are made with your entire arm, not just the forearm or wrist. Small adjustments, which will be covered later, are made in a slightly different manner using the wrist, with the forearm at the same angle as the handle.

Two important notes:

1. The tuning pin is basically a very fine-threaded screw. It can strip or wear out with too much torquing back and forth, and it can also bend, and even snap in half if bent enough.

2. On an upright piano, always hold on to the hammer when it is on a tuning pin. Do not leave the hammer on a pin as a placeholder if you leave the piano. If you are not holding the hammer, it should not be on a pin!

The Tuning Fork

The tuning fork is sounded in the following manner, and ONLY in the following manner:

Hold the very end of the fork with two fingers. Tap one tine onto your kneecap. With practice, you will find which part of the kneecap is the hardest and won't hurt. While the fork is ringing, you can listen to it either by holding it close to your ear, or hold the end against part of the piano, such as the cheek block (the blocks of wood at the ends of the keyboard) or the underside of the keybed.

One common trick is to hold the fork between the index and middle finger, press the end against the underside of the keybed, and then play the note to be tuned with the thumb of that same hand.

Do not hit it against a hard surface or drop it, as this will put the fork out of tune. When buying a fork, buy the most expensive, and therefore highest quality fork you can afford, but make sure that it is smaller than the palm of your hand with the fingers outstretched. You will need two: An "A" fork tuned to 440 cycles per second (cps), and a "C" fork tuned to 523.3 cps. If you get the opportunity, check your fork against a professional tuning machine for accuracy. It can be tuned if necessary by either lightly filing the inside ends of the tines to make it sharper, or the inside crotch of the tines to make it flatter.

NOTE: A tuning fork's accuracy is dependent on it being at room temperature. If cold, it will be sharp. If hot, it will be flat.

The Mutes

You need the following two kinds of mutes in your kit: A rubber mute with a metal handle, and a Papp's Mute.

As you know, each note in a piano may have more than one string. The mute is used for silencing one or two strings so that the strings can be tuned individually, without its unison ringing. It is inserted between the strings you want to silence. The closer to the striking point of the hammer, the more effective it will be.

The Papp's mute is a special mute used in tuning uprights. It is easier than a rubber mute to use when muting strings that are hidden behind the hammers. To insert it, you squeeze the handle gently, and either force it between two side-by-side unisons, or in the middle of three unisons to block the outside strings, or between the outside strings of two adjacent notes.

The Temperament Strip

This is a thick strip of felt, tapered narrower on one end. It is forced between the outside unison strings of two adjacent notes. The felt is inserted starting at the top of the middle section close to the Nut or Agraffe (the termination of the speaking length nearest the tuning pins), and looped over the top of the middle strings to let them ring. Continue looping until you either run out of strings or run out of felt. (I generally carry three strips - one for the treble section in a grand, one for the middle section and one for the bass.) When stripping the bass section, it mutes the left side of one pair, and the right side of the next.

The Mechanics of Tuning

The first step to becoming a good tuner is to master the mechanics of tuning: the use of the hammer, the way the pin reacts to being torqued or turned, and the way the string itself responds.

This, in itself, is probably the most important part of tuning, and the least understood and respected. It is of utmost importance that all tuners understand and master this skill whether they tune by ear or by machine. I have, on many occasions, rescued poor unsuspecting souls who have bought chipping hammers from the local music store thinking that they could tune their own piano. After trying to tune just a few notes, they have broken strings, bent pins, or complained that the pitch doesn't change when they turn the pin.

Here's a nice Canadian analogy to illustrate the process: When you go ice-skating, your skates must be tight in order for you to glide effortlessly and comfortably. You have to tighten the laces from the toe to the top, using a lacing hook to pull each loop as firmly as possible. Then the ends of the laces have to be wound around the upper ankle in the correct way, and tied with a special knot. To skip any of these steps means that your skates will quickly loosen, your ankles will be unsupported, and you'll fall on your face.

When tuning a piano, you have to keep in mind that any movement at the anchor end of the string will mean that the tuning will slip, so you should ensure first of all, that the string is tight to the plate. Then you have to be aware that as you turn the pin to tighten the string, the string may not follow through the agraffe, or over the nut and under the pressure bar at the same rate. Finally, the pin must actually turn in the block, and not just twist on itself.

When you loosen the string, the same forces are in effect, but in reverse. In addition to the above, each two plain string unisons are connected, so you have to make allowances for what effect tightening one side of the unison will have on the other. It is impossible to tune accurately without being aware of, and compensating for, these forces.

The following step-list, although referring to a single string, can be applied to every string. However, it is not the procedure used for pitch raising.

Step-by-Step Process of
Raising and Lowering the Pitch of a String

Ensure that the string is bedded firmly to the plate under the anchor pin. Using a brass rod shaped to a wedge, gently tap each side of the loop at the anchor pin, and tap the string lightly into the crotch of the pin.

(This should be done to all pins the first time you tune a particular piano. If you have done this step previously, or know that it has been done, then skip to the next step.)

Seat the string onto the bridge. Using the end of a hammer shank, tap or rub the string very lightly into the crotch of the bridge pins.

(If the piano is flat and needs a pitch-raise, only tap the string on the non-speaking side of the bridge. After the pitch has been raised, tap the speaking side.)

Make sure that the becket of the string (the bend at the pin) is firmly pushed into the tuning pin hole, and that the coil is tight together.

Put your finger on the key and then play the note. I know that this sounds insanely pedantic, but there are two ways to play a note when tuning: The Soft Blow, and The Hard Blow.

The soft blow is as hard as you can comfortably play the note without lifting your finger from the key.

The hard blow is raising your hand and playing it sharply with two fingers. The soft blow is not soft, however; musically speaking, a soft blow is between mezzo-forte to forte. A hard blow is at least fortissimo. It is important to consistently use the soft blow while tuning, or else the next good player who comes along will put it out of tune with one fortissimo chord.

Change the pitch of the string by gently turning the pin in small nudges. Do not just listen for the sound of the note changing; you must **feel the pin turn** in the pinblock.

If the string was flat in pitch, raise it slightly higher than the desired pitch, release the handle and listen again. It should still be slightly sharp. Give the key a hard blow and listen again. If it is still flat, turn the pin a little more. **It is very important to not over-turn the pin!** Not only will you prematurely loosen the pin, but you will lose stability, not to mention waste time.

Unless the piano has oversized pins, there should be a little play between the tuning hammer tip and the pin. Use this play to gently tap the pin laterally by raising the handle of the hammer while the tip is on the pin and gently tapping the handle down. **Do not bend the pin in any way!**

With new tips, it is sometimes necessary to back the tip a little off of the pin to create a slack space between the tip and the pin. Tapping inside of the slack space is your way of seeing if the string is frozen against the contact points between the speaking length and the tuning pin. This takes a lot of practice, but after a while it becomes an automatic motion.

If the string was sharp, first use the slack-tip tap method to see where the hidden tension of the string is. It might just tap onto pitch. If it doesn't, nudge the pin so that the pitch lowers to just above the desired pitch, play the note with a hard blow and listen again. If it is still sharp, nudge it again. If it is on pitch, slack-tip tap to see if it goes flat. If it does, slack-tip tap upwards, to see if it raises. If it does, leave it on pitch. If it is still flat, nudge the pitch up.

If you encounter a tuning pin that is too loose to adequately hold pitch, mark the tip of the pin with chalk, and test the rest of the pins before you carry on with tuning. The loose pins can then be replaced as a group.

(**NOTE:** *If you notice a number of loose pins in a row or in a cluster, it may indicate a cracked or de-laminated pinblock*).

Conversely, if you encounter pins that are so tight that they "snap" when turning (not literally break, but move with a snapping motion), move the handle of the tuning hammer close to a portion of the piano's case or plate and brace your hand against it when turning the hammer. In this case, the nudging motion does not work. Instead, try to carefully raise the pitch of the string, and then hard blow and tap to set the pin.

The combination of soft blow, hard blow, nudging and tapping, will not only result in a more stable tuning, but it will also save time and energy once it becomes second nature. To simply pull the string up to pitch or to push it down, will not only waste your time, but it is hard on the piano, your body, and your customer's ears. A sure sign of an inexperienced tuner is the sound of a string being raised and lowered over and over.

Hammer Technique 101

Tools Needed For This Section:

1. Short tip Extendable Tuning Hammer
2. Three Rubber Mutes
2. One temperament Strip
3. Two Tuning Forks: A:440 & C:523.3.

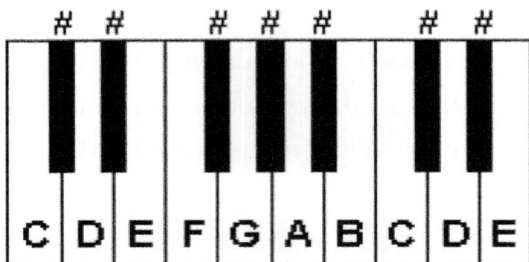

The Keyboard

Exercise #1

Start by inserting rubber mutes so that they block out the right-hand two unisons of A below middle C, the E above middle C, and the A above middle C. Play the fork by hitting it on the knee cap. Play the A above middle C, place the hammer on the pin for the speaking string and try to match that note to the fork.

There are two ways to do this:

You can play the fork, holding the end of the fork between the index and middle fingers of one hand, and then play the note with your thumb and hold the end of the fork against the bottom of the keybed, underneath the note you are holding.

If you are brave, stick the end of the fork between your teeth.

Play the fork, and the A, and listen for a warble or vibrato called "beats".

Remember how fast the beats are, and tune the A below so that it beats the same speed. Then check that note against the fork and tune the A above to the A below.

For the sake of this exercise, just play the note, compare it to the fork, and then tune the string to where you think it will match. Play the fork again and repeat it till the note and the fork are beatless together. When you have done this you can congratulate yourself on completing the first step to learning how to tune.

Give yourself as long as you need to do this step accurately, and then try to do the same thing using the tuning fork in the different ways explained previously.

Remember that Rome wasn't built in a day. Go

slowly, and give yourself plenty of time to master each new section in this book.

Exercise #2

Tune the A above Middle C so that it is beatless with the fork. Now tune the A an octave below so that it is beatless with the A above. Next, tune the E above middle C to the A below so that it is beatless.

Now play the E and the A above at the same time and listen for the beats. Play the E and the A below and compare it to the upper combination of notes.

Notice how the upper two notes beat fast when played together while the lower two are beatless. Now tune the E so that it is beatless with the A above. Try the lower A and the E and listen to the speed of the beats. Now the lower beats fast and the upper is pure.

Now tune the E so that it beats with both the upper A and the lower A at the same rate. Practice matching the beat rates until you can manipulate the pin so that you can make these very minute adjustments.

Exercise #3

Once you have the "feel" of the tuning hammer, check the upper A to make sure that it is beatless to the fork. Tune the E below so that it beats about once per second with the A above, and then tune the A below middle C so that it is beatless with the E. Now, check the A to A octave. Bring the lower A just a little sharper so that you just begin to hear the beat between the two A's slow down to almost nothing. Check the Lower A with the E above and balance the A below so that there is a slightly noticeable beat with the E but practically no beat with the A above.

Finally, check the lower A against the fork. If you have done the above exercise properly, the upper A will be completely beatless with the fork, but the lower A, while not really beating, is not perfectly pure, either.

If this works, then congratulations! You now have not only learned how to manipulate the pin with proper hammer technique, but you have also tempered two notes: the lower A and the E.

It would be best if you could find an established tuner to be a mentor, for there is nothing better than having the instant feedback to correct your mistakes before they become ingrained.

In addition, probably the best way to learn

would be to start with mastering tuning the unisons and the octaves, before tackling the temperament. However, unless you have a temperament set into the piano, practicing the unisons and octaves are nothing more than practicing the mechanics. It is the most important skill to learn, so continue on once you think you have "the feel" of how to set the pin properly, and can do the above exercises fairly effortlessly.

C.H. Musselwhite, Piano Technician.

The Temperament

"Beauty is in the eye of the beholder". The fact of the matter is, when a piano is considered beautifully "in tune", it is actually out of tune in a very precise manner.

To a trained singer, violinist, or for that matter any instrumentalist who does not use a keyboard of some type, this "out-of-tune-ness" is not only obvious to them, but they have to learn to accept it as the "standard sound" of a tuned piano.

At the other extreme, people learn to accept the sound of an un-tuned, or poorly tuned piano as well.

As a professional piano tuner, it is part of our job to not only tune well, but to teach our customers the importance of having their piano properly tuned, and keeping it in tune.

Over the past four centuries, a lot of very brilliant musical minds have given us not only the amazing instrument/machine/art called a piano, but have established what the sound of the piano should be. If we are charged with preserving their legacies, it behooves us to take this task seriously and professionally, and master this "Art of Compromise".

It is interesting to note that to the player, the most noticeable (and therefore the most important) parts of the tuning are, in order: the unisons; then the octaves; and finally, the temperament.

The layman will instantly recognize when a unison is out of tune, but rarely notice when the temperament is poorly set. To the tuner, however, the opposite is the case: The temperament is of utmost importance; then the octaves (and the stretch); then, last but not least, the unisons.

As explained in the introduction, the temperament is an attempt to squeeze twelve semitones plus the Pythagorean comma into the space of twelve steps: thirteen into twelve.

It is as if we were building a staircase twelve feet high, but were instructed to use thirteen risers. Each step, therefore, would be 9.23076" high instead of ten inches. However, even after carefully measuring and cutting, when assembled, we find that the staircase is still a fraction of an inch too high. To correct this, we either have to shorten one or two steps to make it fit, or carefully shorten each step by an infinitesimal but equal amount. Historical (unequal) temperaments are like the first solution, while the equal temperament is like the latter.

Each semitone has to be made slightly smaller than a perfect semitone in order for twelve semitones to equal an octave.

Unlike the staircase example, the Pythagorean comma is not a full step. In technical terms, the difference between semi-tones is measured in units known as cents. We say that an increase of a semitone in pitch on the piano keyboard equals 100 cents. However, a pure semitone, mathematically, is exactly 101.95 cents. Therefore, the extra "step" that we have to squeeze into the twelve steps of the scale is 23.5 cents, or a little less than a quartertone. *(It's actually 23.46 cents, but I've rounded everything up.)* Each note we tune has to be 1.95 cents off of perfect to compensate for the extra 23.5 cents that has to be included in the octave.

In order to properly explain the techniques involved in setting the temperament, a little clarification of terminology is necessary: First of all, the names of the keys.

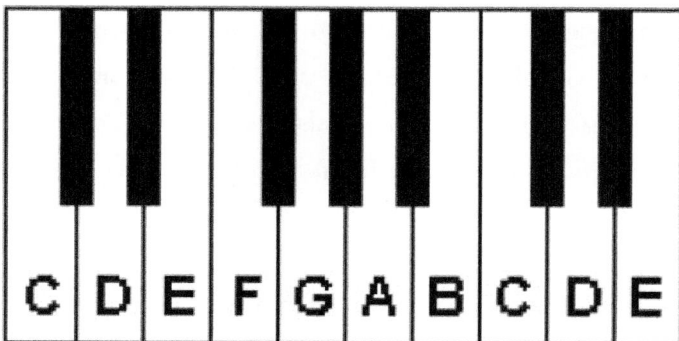

The black notes above the white notes are named "sharp" (#) e.g. the black note above the note C is C Sharp (C#). Musically speaking, the black notes below the white notes are named "flat" (b). However, a black note is only referred to as "flat" in the context of music. A semitone (the musical step between one key to the next whether black or white) is referred to in music as a minor second or "m2". Two semitones, or a whole tone, is a Major second or "M2". Note that the "M" is capitalized when Major. (Please refer to the chart on the next page.)

The Keyboard Intervals

Starting at the top left corner and going down, you see the intervals in chromatic order. If you look across the top row, you will see an example of the sequence of Major thirds used in The Augmented Chord Check discussed on p.25. As you can see, the naming of the intervals is not completely straightforward. Some intervals, the fourth, fifth and octave, are called Perfect (even though on the piano they are not), and what would logically be called a minor fifth is referred to as a diminished fifth. The reason for these terms stem from their use in music, but what is important is that you memorize the names of these intervals and learn to recognize their sound.

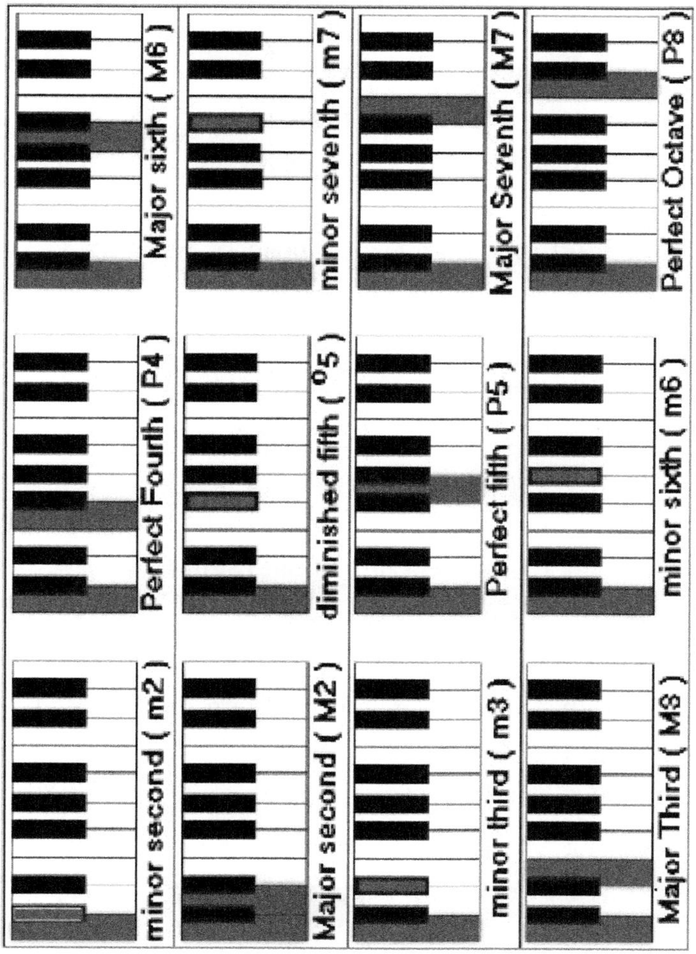

Many music students use a little trick to learn the sound of intervals – they associate an interval with a song.

For example: The first two notes in "My Bonnie Lies Over The Ocean" are a Major sixth. The first two notes of the theme from "Love Story" are a minor sixth. It is important to note that the "Perfect" intervals, the fourth, fifth and octave, are beatless when they are "perfect"ly in tune with each other, or what tuners would describe as "Pure" intervals. When we temper the tuning of the piano, we alter these pure intervals in order to include the Pythagorean Comma.

For example, let's use two notes on the keyboard: The F below middle C and the G below middle C. To compensate for the comma, we need to bring these two notes closer together by 3.9 cents. If we tune the C above these two notes to a tuning fork, we can use this note as a reference. From this C down to the F is a Perfect fifth (P5). From the C down to the F is a Perfect fourth (P4). The sound of a pure perfect fifth is rather ingrained into the ears of western civilization. From the drone of a bagpipe, to the chanting of a medieval chorus, our ears "know" the sound of a pure fifth, so we strive to make this interval as clean as possible, while still less than perfect.

The sound of a perfect fourth is less ingrained,

but still recognizable, so we can alter the interval more than we can alter the fifth without making musically trained ears uncomfortable.

3.9 cents less than perfect, however, is still a big enough difference as to be easily recognized by the trained ear. So, we compensate by making the fifth slightly smaller, and the fourth slightly bigger. If we made both smaller, it would cancel the comma, and if we made both bigger it would increase the comma.

To keep the fifth sounding pure-ish, we give it less error than we do the fourth. Tuners use the term "Narrow" to describe an interval made smaller or closer together, and the term "Wide" to describe an Interval made bigger or farther apart.

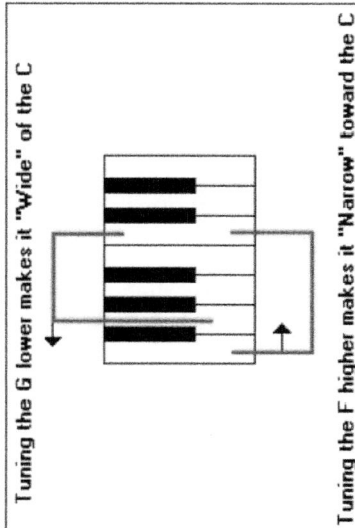

Although there are many ways to set the temperament, we will start with a series of intervals known as the "Circle of Fourths and Fifths". This pattern is sometimes referred to as "Chasing the Tail".

An Important Note About Time: It is not unusual for beginning tuners to spend hours trying to tune a piano. This is a very difficult and frustrating process for most people, and many give up and use an electronic tuner to bypass the agony of learning. Don't despair, be patient with yourself!

The two keys to learning anything new are:

1. **Interest**. If you have the interest, you have the motivation, which is the most important thing you need.
2. **Simplification**. Anything can be broken up into smaller bits, and smaller bits are easier to grasp.

In the initial learning stage, don't worry about tuning the whole piano. Concentrate on tuning ONE string, then ONE unison set, then ONE octave, etc.

Your goal is to eventually be able to tune a piano within about an hour. In order to do that, you have to master the steps along the way and become faster at each step. This is the main way to increase speed. With practice you should be able to set the temperament within ten minutes or so. That's it! Don't worry about any other part of the tuning as a whole. Setting the temperament is only about 10% of the total task, so strive toward doing an "okay" job within about ten minutes time.

Remember: *The customer will be more concerned about how well your unisons are set. As you become better at all the skills, your quality will improve automatically. Don't let yourself fall into the trap of striving for perfection first. Instead, strive for efficiency.*

I am often asked how I tune a piano so quickly. The secret is threefold.

First: Skill with the hammer acquired over time.

Second: The ability to hear quickly when something is right, and not second-guess yourself. (As my Dad often said: "If it's not broke, don't fix it!").

Thirdly: (And this is where the majority of tuners are challenged), **Don't Waste Time**. Don't check if it's not necessary, and don't waste time fiddling around, playing unnecessary runs, trills or catchy little ditties. Save your playing of the piano until the end, when it will seem like a reward for finishing.

Playing a lot during the tuning can seem to a listener like vanity and procrastination, while being efficient with the process will make the customer feel that you are truly a professional.

temperament Pattern #1 - "Chasing the Tail"

First, insert a temperament strip between the unison sets of each note so that it mutes the outside strings of each set from at least the E below middle C to the G above middle C.

NOTE: Always press down the damper pedal when inserting the strip. The action of inserting the strip can move the strings together, which could damage the damper felt.

Start by tuning the middle C to a tuning fork tuned to C: 523.3 beats per minute (bpm.). Compare the fork to the C above middle C and listen to the speed of the beats between the note on the piano and the fork. Determine if it is sharp or flat of the fork.

Now, tune the middle C so that it beats to the C above at the same rate. Next, check the middle C with your fork. If it is beatless, then you have successfully tuned that note. Listen to the note for at least four or five seconds. If middle C beats against the fork, then you misjudged the direction (sharp or flat) that you altered middle C.

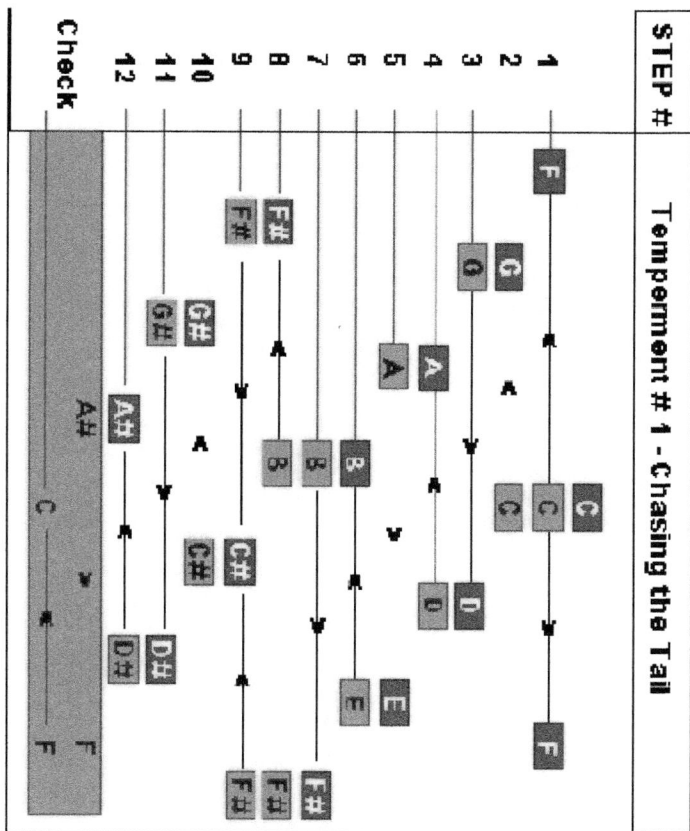

STEP 1: Once middle C is in tune, play it and the F below middle C at the same time.

(Remember that although this interval is called a perfect fifth, to temper the F it must be sharp of perfect or "narrow".)

Bring the note so that it is absolutely beatless, and then raise it sharp to the point where it just starts to beat. Somewhere between beatless and beating is a spot where the beats are described as "just rolling over". It is so slow as to be imperceptible unless you listen to these two notes for three or more seconds.

Now, tune the F above middle C, using the F an octave below. Every time you tune an octave, keep in mind that you are stretch tuning, and the octaves are not exactly pure.

This particular octave, called the temperament Octave, is the purest in the whole piano, but still the goal is to make the upper F sharper than the lower F WITHOUT HEARING A BEAT. I know this sounds impossible on paper, but in practice, you will soon find that there is a very small range of play to the octaves where it can be slightly under or over without hearing any beats.

Test the upper F to the middle C, and make sure that it beats at least as fast as your heartbeat. (Check your pulse on the carotid artery of your neck as a reference.) If you can't make the C-F P4 beat, then either your FF P8 is too pure or narrow, or your F-C P5 is too slow.

STEP 2: Now, tune the G below middle C to the C. This "Perfect Fourth" should beat exactly the same as the C F P4. An important point to note here is that the slower your fifths are, the faster your fourths will have to be.

STEP 3: Tune the D above middle C to the G you just tuned, keeping the fifth narrow.

STEP 4: Tune the A a fourth down from the D. It is at this point that you will be able to check if your fifths and fourths are beating at the right rate. Play the F-C P5 and listen for the slow rollover. Now play the D-G P5 and compare the speed of the rollover to the first P5.

It is very important to take your time here; there is a time and place for speed and THIS IS NOT IT!

Now check the speed of the C-G P4 to the D-A P4. Their beat rates must match exactly. Finally, play the F-A M3. It should beat around 6-7 bps, or about as fast as you can *easily* say wah-wah-wah-wah-wah-wah-wah. If it is beating too slowly, then either your fourths are beating too fast, or your fifths are too pure. Check your fourths and fifths again. If you're certain that they are right, then **continue on to the next step**.

NOTE: There is a natural tendency to try to make the fourths too pure. Keep in mind that it is possible to tune the fifths perfect, and the fourths quite fast, and still end up making everything basically equal. This kind of temperament results in a huge stretch and is often used by concert tuners to make a piano sound brighter and more exciting in a large reverberant place such as a cathedral.

Doing the opposite, tuning the fifths and fourths beating equally, gives you a less lively-sounding piano. This "blended" temperament is the type of temperament found in electronic keyboards, and although acceptable, it is important that you know the sound of narrow fifths and wide fourths before the more advanced temperaments are explained. Without almost pure fifths, it is difficult to adequately do the stretch tuning covered later.

Now we continue this pattern of fourths and fifths until we end up back at middle C.

STEP 5: Tune the E from the A below.

STEP 6: Tune the B from the A.

STEP 7: Next, tune the F# above middle C from the B below.

STEP 8: Tune the F# an octave below. Make sure that when tuning this octave, that you tune the lower F# so that it is slightly wide and beats properly with the B a P4 above.

STEP 9: Tune the C# to the lower F#, checking it with the upper F# P4.

STEP 10: Tune the G# a P4 below the C#.

STEP 11: Tune the D# to the G#.

STEP 12: Tune A# to the D# P4.

Stop there! Don't check the A#-F P5, but rather go back to the beginning and make sure that every fourth and fifth are beating properly. Play the F-C P5, and then go up in semitones very slowly (F#-C#, G-D, G#-D#, etc.). They should all have the same beat rate. Now do the same thing with the P4's (F-A#, F#-B, etc.) You should be able to check them by playing each succeeding interval after a little more than a second for each chord. In other words, you should hear the beat a second after playing the interval, move up, hear the next beat, and so on. They must have the same beat rate. If they don't, you have to start again and fix any mistakes you might have made along the way.

Now we get to the interesting part: Play the F

above middle C and the P5 down to the A#. If it doesn't beat the same as the other fifths, then memorize how fast the interval is beating, and figure out if the A# is sharp or flat by tapping up or down. If all the P5's and P4's are beating at the right rate, and constant in speed from one P4 to the next, etc., then you can figure out quite easily where you went wrong in your "Staircase-Building Compromise".

If the A# is sharp of where it should be, your P4's are beating too slowly. If the A# is flat or not beating at all, your P4's are beating too fast. Play the P4's and take a good guess as to how fast they should be beating, in order to go through the whole thing again and end up at the right place.

Here's a little hint: You'll probably be way off! This temperament pattern, because it goes in a circle back to the beginning, makes it very easy to multiply small mistakes into a bad finishing interval.

The only way to prevent this happening is to test your progress along the way by using what tuners refer to as "checks".

Play the F below middle C and the A above it. This M3 should be beating about 6-7 beats per second (bps.) If the A#-F P5 is beating about this fast, the amount you will have to change each P4 amounts to about less than .5 bps. This is such a small amount that you probably won't be able to change all the P4's to compensate for that amount, without getting clues to "check" your progress along the way.

temperament Pattern #2 - "Beating around the Bush"

Here is a slight alternative to "Chasing the Tail" that incorporates quite a few handy checks. I call it "Beating around the Bush".

It starts exactly like the pattern explained in the previous section. Do the pattern again starting with the heading labeled, "temperament Pattern #1". When you reach the place where it says: "**continue on to the next step**", continue on below.

STEP 5: At this point, we have tuned Middle C, F below, G below, A below D above, and the F above.

Tune the C# above middle C so that the A-C# M3 is faster than the F-A M3, and the C#-F M3 is faster still. Think of the C# as being halfway between the A and the F, but a little closer to the A.

(We'll get back to this note again later in this temperament pattern, but it's good to have it close to use as a reference.)

When you believe that the C# sounds right, then tune the F# a P5 below, and the F# a P4 above.

Remember to get the beat rates right, and tune the octave a hair narrow. You shouldn't exactly hear any beating, but it still can't be a perfect "Perfect Octave".

STEP 6: Tune the B between the two F#'s.

STEP 7: Tune the A# so that it beats with the F# M3 below just a shade faster than the F-A M3.

If everything has gone well, you now have one of the most useful checks available to you: The Augmented Chord Check.

Play the following series of two-note M3 chords: F-A, then A-C#, then C#-F. Each M3 should beat slightly faster than the one before it. Now play F#-A#, A#-D, then D-F#. Again, each M3 should beat faster than the one before it. Now play F-A, F#-A#, A-C#, A#-D, C#-F, and D-F#. This sequence can tell you an awful lot about where you have gone wrong, if you have gone wrong at all.

As always, the farther up the scale chromatically a third is, the faster it should beat. M3's a semitone apart should be quite close in speed, though, enough for you to see if they are indeed speeding up.

Now check the A# below middle C to the P5 F above. Remember that the A# should be slightly sharp of perfect, making a narrow fifth that should just roll over slowly. Play the A#-D M3, and listen to the beat rate. Now, play the A-C# M3. It should be just a little slower. If it's not, then tune the C# again so that it is in the middle beat-wise between the A and the F.

Now, when you play the following sequence, each third should beat faster than the third below: F-A

M3, A-C# M3, and C#-F M3.

Now, try the A-C# M3 and the A#-D M3. The higher a third is chromatically, the faster it should beat. If this does not happen, check all the fifths you have tuned to make sure they sound the same. Then, check the fourths.

The most common cause for things not working out in this pattern is having one or two of the notes beating in the wrong direction; i.e. the A in the A-D P4 tuned narrow instead of wide. Remember: The fifths are narrow and the fourths are wide. **A narrow fourth can still have the same beat rate as a wide fourth.**

STEP 8: With all the checks explained previously, we should be pretty certain that the A# is right. Use it to tune the D# a P4 above. We can now use the Augmented Chord Check on that D#. Play the GB M3, then the B-D# M3. If the upper third is faster, then continue on.

STEP 9: Tune the E above middle C using the A a P5 below, the B a P4 below, and check it with the C an M3 below. With so many notes to check it to, it should be fairly clear where it should be.

STEP 10: Tune the G# below middle C using the D#

above, or the C#. (Or, for that matter, any other note you want.)

If you have done everything properly, they're all in tune! Congratulations, you can now use the Augmented Check on all the notes in the temperament.

temperament Pattern #3 – Diefenbaugh

Now that you have explored the two rudimentary temperament patterns (and hopefully have the sound of the escalating thirds planted firmly in your mind), we'll explore the concept of temperaments at a slightly more advanced level, and look at using thirds as tuning intervals rather than as just checks.

This pattern is called the "Diefenbaugh" because it was named after its biggest proponent and probable inventor, George Diefenbaugh, the former head of the Service Department for Kawai USA Inc.

The first big difference is that we'll use an A: 440 fork, rather than the C. Tune the A above middle C so that it precisely matches the fork, and then tune the A below middle C so it is on the wide side of beatless.

STEP 1: Tune the F below middle C to the lower A so that it does the normal 6-7 bps (wah-wah, etc.).

STEP 2: Tune the F above middle C to the F below. (Fifths narrow, fourths wide!)

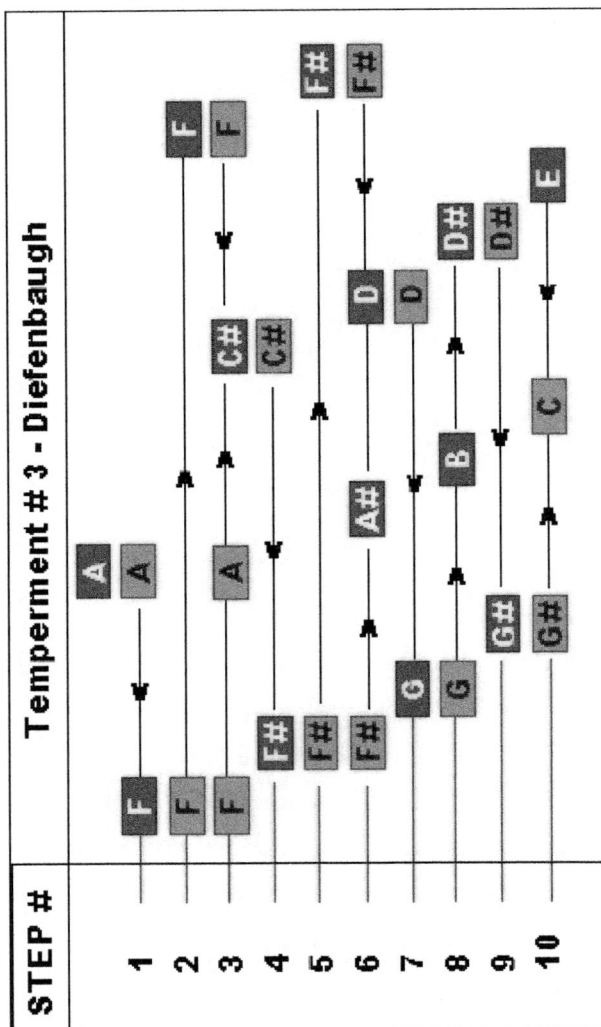

STEP 3: Tune the C# so that it beats slightly faster to the F than it does to the A. You can now do the Augmented Check F-A, A-C#, C#-F. Make sure that each third gets faster as you play the higher chord.

STEP 4: Tune the F# below middle C to the C#.

STEP 5: Tune the F# above to the F# below.

STEP 6: Using the F#'s, tune the A# and the D. You now have many other checks you can do to test these two notes.

STEP 7: Now tune the G below middle C to the D.

STEP 8: Using thirds, tune the B and the D#. There are a lot of tests you can do here, as well.

STEP 9: Tune the G# below middle C using thirds (or any other applicable interval - there are quite a few.)

STEP 10: Tune the E above middle C. Remember that you started with an A fork, so it should be VERY obvious if you have done this temperament pattern properly.

temperament Pattern #4 - Thirds and Fifths

Just in case you wanted another option similar to the Diefenbaugh, here is a temperament pattern only using thirds and fifths. (Of course, you can always use fourths as checks along the way).

I use this pattern when I am pitch raising, or if I'm in a big hurry. With practice it can give you a decent-sounding temperament very quickly - if you're not too fussy about what the fourths sound like!

As I mentioned earlier, it is very important when you are just learning to tune the temperament that you don't rush. The standard principle to learning anything new is two steps forward, and one step back. Push yourself towards speed and efficiency, but don't skip steps, and don't rush.

New tuners often spend an hour or more putting a good temperament down, but it is with time and practice that speed and accuracy comes, not by rushing the learning process. With practice, you will eventually be able to lay a good temperament in less than ten minutes, but don't be frustrated with how long a tuning is taking. With practice and patience, your speed will increase and your accuracy will improve.

Temperment #4 - Thirds and Fifths

temperament Pattern # 5
The "Blended" temperament.

I rarely use this style of temperament, but it has its uses. It is most similar to the type of tempering found in electronic keyboards, and many of the electronic tuners that I have tested.

It results in fourths and fifths that are fairly close in speed, which makes a satisfying stretch difficult to lay down, and gives the piano a less exciting sound. However, it has one huge benefit: Using this concept, thirds and sixths have roughly the same beat speed, which means that you have more checks available, and these checks are very easy to hear.

The basic concept here is that even though the fifths are narrow and the fourths wide, they are basically the same speed: a slightly faster roll-over than we normally put in the fifths is also used in the fourths. It is too slow to count accurately, but it is noticeable when the fourths are too fast compared to each other.

The pattern starts like the thirds and fifths pattern explained previously. The trick here is to make sure that you are compromising EVERY interval but the octave. In other words, no interval will be even close to beatless (except the octave).

The best thing about this temperament is that

the M3 and the M6 above any given note will have the same beat rate and will progress evenly as they rise chromatically in pitch. If you know what you are listening for, it doesn't matter which pattern you use.

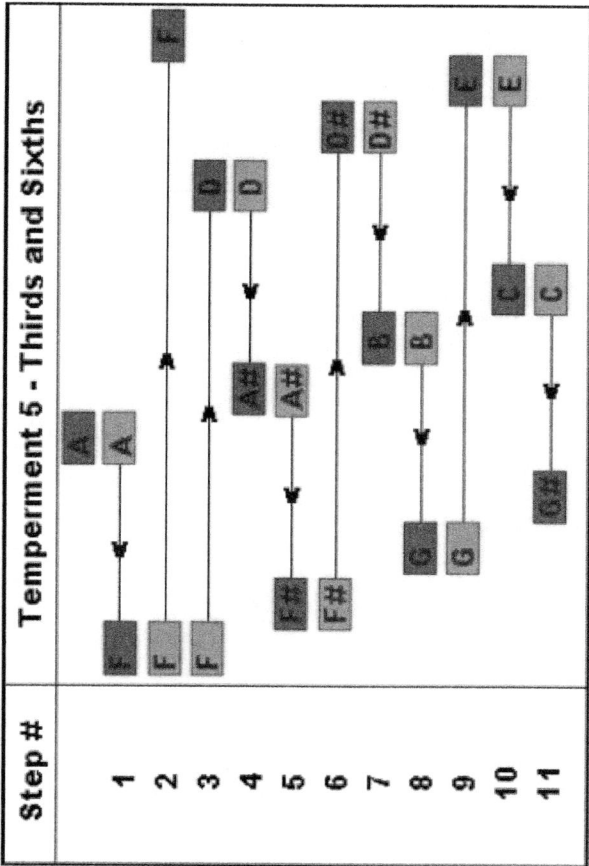

temperament Pattern #6 - The 6-3-3

Every pattern is just a tool to help you hear how you are tempering each note. This pattern is one of my favourites. Not only does it work well and sound nice, but it also has a lot of checks built in, and is very easy to remember when you are starting out.

After setting the A and the two F's, you tune a sixth up and then two thirds down. Then, another sixth up, and two thirds down – hence, the nickname, "The 6-3-3".

The other interesting part of this pattern is that every interval is tuned wide.

STEPS 1&2: First, set the A to your fork, then tune the F an M3 down (6-7 bps -wah-wah, etc.), then the A below middle C so that it is wide, and then the F a P8 above.

This is where the fun really starts.

STEP 3: Tune the D a P6 up from the F sharp, so that it beats exactly the same speed as the F-A M3. (Technically, the interval of the sixth should beat a tiny bit faster, but it is easier while you are still learning if you match the beat rate.)

STEP 4: Tune the A# a P3 down from the D so that it beats a little faster than the F-A M3. You can then check the A# against the two F's on either side to make sure that they beat roughly the same.

(Because of scaling differences in some pianos, you may have to make the P4's beat slightly faster than the P5's, but you don't have to be too picky at this point.)

STEP 5: Tune the F# an M3 below the A# you just tuned so that it beats slightly faster than the F-A M3, but slower than the A#-D M3. At this point it will be obvious if your A# is not right.

STEP 6: Tune the D# a P6 up from the F# so that it beats the same speed as the F#-A# M3.

STEP 7: Tune the B an M3 down from the D# you just tuned, so that it beats slightly faster than the A#-D M3.

STEP 8: Tune the G an M3 down from the B. You can now do the Augmented Chord Check covered previously in this chapter. You can also check this G to the P5 - D above.

STEP 9: Tune the E a P6 up so that it beats the same speed as the G-B M3.

STEP 10: Tune the C an M3 down from the E.

STEP 11: Tune the G# an M3 down from the C. To use this pattern to make a normal stretch temperament, make the sixths beat about 7-8 bps compared to the M3's 6-7 bps. Temper the octaves slightly wide, and when you check the fourths and fifths, make the fifths as clean as possible.

Troubleshooting your Temperament

Everyone struggles with the temperament. Even seasoned tuners can have an "off" day, or encounter a piano that seems to fight the process from beginning to end. However, a couple of quick pointers can save you some grief.

Many small pianos have extremely compromised scaling which can cause problems in tuning. If you have to tune a piano where the trichords start in the middle of the temperament octave, you can be sure that setting the initial notes are going to be tricky. One way to solve this is to set the temperament in a higher register; however, this takes some practice.

Another simpler way is to take your best guess, and then duplicate the temperament an octave up.

Mute the whole mid-section, tune the temperament, and then tune the G-G P8, the G#-G# P8, etc. As you tune, check the fourths and fifths as you go.

If you have made an error lower down, it will multiply itself higher up, making it easier to spot and to fix. Just fix the error up high, and then transfer the fix to the lower octave.

The same solutions can be applied if you have trouble setting the temperament in any given piano. Just tune the temperament over two octaves and make note of where the error reproduces itself.

For instance: Say the problem stems from you making the E above middle C slightly flat. As soon as you tune the A below middle C to the A above, the fourth will be beating way too fast. Simply lower the E, and suddenly, the E-A P4 is beating at the right speed.

As I have said earlier, if your temperament isn't perfect, chances are that most people won't hear the problem. This isn't to say that you can do a sloppy job every time; instead, it means that you can relax about trying to be perfect, and just do the best job you can with the time that you have. The next time you tune, you will do better. Practice does make perfect.

The most common error in setting the

temperament is having an interval beat at the right speed but tuned in the wrong direction.

If you set the interval perfect first, and then make it narrow or wide, you will avoid this problem. If you get to the end and things don't work out, first check the beat rates by comparing an ascending series of perfect fifths, i.e.: F-C P5, F#-C# P5, G-D P5, etc. Or perfect fourths, or Major thirds, or Major sixths. (Practice playing these series of intervals until you can do them smoothly and confidently.)

If you don't hear a problem, then check the direction of the interval spread by going through the temperament pattern again, and slack-tip tap each note lightly to test which way they are tuned.

Problem Solving

Sometimes it can seem as if the entire career of tuning is an exercise in problem solving, but to many people, problem solving is the spice of life.

Setting the temperament is a lot like doing a crossword puzzle - a pleasurable pastime rather than a chore. Every clue you get, gives you a clue toward the solution. If you pay attention, you will soon notice that one mistake you made early in the pattern has affected something later on; an interval near the end; a slow third in the middle of the ascending Major third check; an octave that doesn't work with a P5. Instead of ignoring the signs, check back and see where you might have gone wrong. Think of it as doing the crossword in pencil, and erasing a wrong answer. As soon as you take away the wrong one, sometimes the right one presents itself!

The Octaves

Tuning the octaves is much more than playing an octave above and tuning two notes together. Each octave away from the temperament is tempered itself, not only to achieve a "stretch" tuning, but also to align the note each note you are tuning to the harmonic sequence inherent in each individual note.

The Harmonic Sequence

Re-read this quote from the introduction to this book:

"If you play a string, and then divide it in half by placing your finger on the middle of the string (what physicists call "the node"), you would hear a note one octave higher than the first note, which is called the 'Fundamental'. (If you play middle C on a piano, and the C above it that is in tune, that is an octave.)

If you then divide that half in half again, you would hear a 'Perfect Fifth' above the Octave. (Like playing C and the G above it.) If you continued to subdivide the string in this manner, you would hear a rather mysterious thing: a note two octaves higher, then a third (C to E) above that, then the fifth, then a minor 7th (C to A#), then all the diatonic notes (like all the white keys), and then every single note.

If you could go even further, you would hear microtones, which are not part of the western scale, but which are a part of the music of other cultures."

You can experiment with this in real life. You need a grand piano, preferably one that is in tune.

Play the C, two octaves below middle C, and check the tuning of that note against the octave above. Hopefully it will be a reasonably pure octave. Now, find the middle of that string while it vibrates, and hold your finger lightly against the string. Now play it repeatedly while you move the position of your finger up and down the string until you clearly hear the first harmonic (the C an octave above the note you are playing). Check the tuning of that harmonic against the octave. You should be able to hear a slight difference in the beat rate.

Now, check against two octaves above, and

three octaves, etc. Each octave will have a different beat rate. If you take the time to tune all those octaves pure, and then re-tune them to match the harmonic you'll notice that the harmonic is definitely sharp of the fundamental - the note you are playing, rather than the harmonic.

The spot where you are touching the string is called the first node. If you move your finger closer toward you on the string, you will find the other higher nodes. If you test the tuning of these harmonics, you will find that they are even sharper than the first.

The reason why there are not as many dampers as there are strings, is so that the upper strings will ring sympathetically with the lower strings. However, these strings will only vibrate if they are excited by another vibration in the same pitch harmonically. Therefore, in order to set the upper strings ringing, they have to line up tuning-wise with the harmonics of the lower strings.

The only way to do that is to tune them sharp. They won't ring with the fundamentals of the lower notes because their own fundamentals start too high.

The sound of a piano is greatly affected by the acoustics of the room, and the ability of the soundboard to reproduce the sounds of the strings. If a piano is in a small dead room, the effect of a high stretch can be too apparent in the octaves. In a large reverberant room, you can stretch the octaves to a truly ridiculous point before it will become apparent to a listener at the other end of the room. The big stretch in the big room will excite the upper strings and make the piano stand out. However, a big stretch in a small room may make the upper strings resonate, but it will also make the stretched octaves annoying to the listener.

Therein lies another part of the Art of Compromise, and another reason why aural tuning is superior: Every piano has to be tuned differently - and tuned differently in every space - in order for it to sound its best. There is no magic formula for determining how much to stretch the octaves. The only way to correctly determine it is to let the piano tell you, and for you to hear it.

To Strip or Not to Strip

I strip every note on the piano in a grand, and everything except the treble in an upright. It is because, in essence, what I am doing in the stretch is extending the temperament to each end of the keyboard. It is easier to do the same kinds of checks as in the temperament octave higher up, or lower down, if you don't have to worry about your unisons while you tune the octaves.

Personally, I don't see any reason why not to do this. It's not as if not stripping saves time; the time you save not inserting the strip will probably be small, compared to the time you waste getting the octaves and unisons to line up properly with the temperament octave.

There is another reason to strip:

If, when the strip is in, you still hear the muted unisons because they are so far out of tune, then you know instantly that the piano needs a pitch raise.

Back when I used a rubber mute to tune past the temperament, I would sometimes get halfway through the treble or bass before I realized that that section of the piano was so flat as to not be stable. It was a bit of an embarrassing situation to inform the customer at that point in the process that my fee had suddenly gone up.

If you strip first, set the pitch of the piano, and quickly play the keyboard chromatically, it will be very apparent if the piano needs a pitch raise.

When you strip the bass section, make note of the pattern that you have to make in skipping from pin to pin with the hammer. It is always symmetrical, so you don't have to waste time figuring out where to put your hammer for the next string.

There will be an easily followed pattern if you

look for it. Often the muted strings are the "inside" pins in a set of four. In some pianos, the ringing strings go: Left up, right down, skip two, etc. After you have some experience under your belt in recognizing all these patterns, tuning a stripped bass is no more difficult then tuning a stripped treble.

Order of Tuning

There is a specific order that the octaves should be tuned so that you balance the change of stress over the entire scale.

First, tune upwards until you are one octave into the top section. (If you tune past this point, the chances are great that you will have to retune the upper octaves once you have finished the bass section.)

As a whole, the wound strings are under greater tension than either section of plain strings. Additionally, the shorter the string, the less movement is needed to change its pitch. Therefore, as you tune the lower sections you add or subtract stress to the piano. In some pianos, this can cause a large enough movement to alter the pitch of the higher, shorter strings. This is because the strings press down on the soundboard, which is convex. As you raise the pitch of the strings, you increase the amount of downward pressure on the soundboard.

After you have finished the first octave of the top section, tune downwards into the bass until you reach the lowest note. After that, the temperament strip is pulled out note by note until the top of the middle section.

Before continuing to tune the unisons further, the octaves in the top section should be checked for a change in pitch.

The Stretch

Here are two quick little exercises to illustrate the concept of stretch tuning:

Start with a piano that is tune. Strip the mid-section of the piano, and tune the C an octave below middle C so that it is beatless to your fork. Now, tune the G a P5 above the lower C so that it is pure. Tune the D a P5 up from the G so that it is pure, and finally, tune the A a P5 up from the D also pure. Now compare the A against your A tuning fork. You should notice that it beats about 4 bps. That is the difference between pure octaves, and tempered octaves.

For the next exercise it is best to have a grand piano at your disposal.

Play the second lowest A on the keyboard and

subdivide the string with your finger so that it rings the second harmonic - the E below middle C. Play the key hard so that the harmonic is very strong and at the same time, play the E below middle C and listen to the speed of the beats.

Under ideal circumstances (the right piano and the right space), it is possible to tune the stretch so that the harmonics actually are the same pitch, as in the first example, so that purely tuned fifths can actually be used, rather than the purely tuned octaves. However, ideal circumstances rarely present themselves. Instead, we try to strike a balance so that although we may not be hitting the harmonics dead-on, we are at least in the ballpark.

This is not as hard to do as it may seem, but like everything else it takes practice. In theory, you will simply try to strike a balance between a pure-sounding fifth and a pure-sounding octave, and try to make each octave above and below the temperament beat purely to the temperament octave.

In practice, it is often hard to hear the difference between a pure double or triple octave and one that is flat or sharp. The trick is to use checks, just as we did in the temperament.

After you have stripped the whole piano and set your temperament, begin the octaves by tuning the first note after the temperament (i.e. the G above middle C.) Tune this note and the rest of its octave by setting each note sharp of perfect to the point where the fifths are as pure as possible, but the octave does not beat noticeably.

When you reach the C above middle C, check it with the double fifth or "Twelfth", which is the bottom F in the temperament octave. Ideally you should be able to make this interval beatless without causing too much activity in the octave and fifth.

Because of the distance between these two notes, you will need both hands to play, so you cannot actually use this interval to tune. However, as you continue up, using the octave and the fifth, keep checking the twelfth for purity.

Once you reach the G two octaves above middle C, you will have to start to make the octaves beat more noticeably in order to make the fifths pure. This isn't a problem; in fact, you can probably increase the purity of the fifth and the twelve without the octaves sounding unacceptable.

The goal is, as you tune farther away from the middle of the keyboard, you keep trying to match the note you are tuning with its match in the temperament octave whether in the treble or in the bass. As you go, make sure you are checking these larger intervals rather than relying on the octave. Use it as a reference, but don't try to make it perfect.

If you encounter a note that sounds good with the temperament octave, but screams with the Perfect Octave, make sure that you haven't made a mistake earlier on.

Everything should progress evenly as you go. If something sticks out, then it is a clue that something earlier is wrong.

Octave Tuning in the High Treble

In the last octave, a note tuned pure to the octave below is more likely to be perceived as flat to the trained ear than if it is actually tuned sharp of perfect.

An easy way to tune the section is to raise it very sharp of the octave, and play its corresponding note in the temperament octave. Give the note a hard blow and check. If it is still sharp, slack-tip tap it down a tiny bit, give it a hard blow, and check it again.

It takes such a microscopic movement in the tension of these short strings to change pitch, that often you can literally pound them onto pitch. This, of course, is provided that you raised the note a reasonable amount.

After a few notes, you should be able to roughly

guess how sharp to raise the note so that two or three hard blows set it in place.

Octave Tuning in the Low Bass

This is the most common problem area for beginning tuners.

It is very easy in the beginning to so misjudge the pitch of the bottom octave strings (especially in small pianos), that you could accidentally raise the pitch many semitones too sharp. This could cause the windings in the string to loosen, or the string to break.

The short, low bass strings can give a mirage of beatlessness, especially if they are double-wound. The reason for this has to do with the effect of scaling on harmonics.

You have probably heard that the bigger the piano, the better the sound. This has nothing to do with volume. A string's pitch is determined by three factors: its speaking length, its thickness, and its tension. To get a short bass string to sound the same pitch as its corresponding note in a large string, these factors have to be altered. To decrease the tension would cause a loss of tone, so therefore, the string is made thicker. The thicker the string, the more stiff it becomes.

Tone is dependent on the string vibrating in

smooth oscillations called sine waves. At certain points of the string, called "nodes", these waves double. When you place your finger on the string to hear the harmonics, you are actually touching a node point. In between the node points the vibrating string creates a

Wave Partial

Node

super-oscillation called a wave partial. When a string is stiff, it inhibits the proper formation of the wave partials causing their node points to not line up. This causes each of the super-oscillations to form their own partials.

When a bass string is wildly off-pitch, you can get that illusion of beatlessness because you are hearing a false-partial line up with your reference note. To avoid making a big mistake in the bass, sub-divide each string with your finger to hear the first partial, and go down the scale in semitones. Check each note against the octave or double octave to ensure that it is close to being on pitch. Now when you tune, you know that only a small adjustment is needed to tune each string.

A very common mistake that many tuners make, whether new or experienced, is to hear the quite clear alignment when the string is in tune with the octave above. To make the stretch, you have to lower it below this point.

On most pianos you will actually hear a new beat pattern appear which will slow down to nothing as the twelfth partial begins to coincide with the temperament octave. If it sounds too flat to you at this point, sub-divide the string and listen to the harmonic. It should match the same note played in the temperament.

Sometimes, the acoustics of the piano and the room make this stretch too obvious. In that case, compromise a little towards perfect so that the harmonic aligns with the double octave.

The Unisons

Proper tuning of the unisons is crucial, for practically every customer will be annoyed by poor unisons, and they are often the first thing that slips in a poor tuning.

Problems in unison tuning often occur in the bichords of the bass and the upper trichords in the treble. Loose or poorly made windings, or poor scaling, can cause unisons in wound strings to sound out-of-tune even if they are not - as can false beats in the treble. Therefore, a good tuner must be prepared to deal with these potential problems as part of the tuning procedure.

As was stated earlier, the unisons are tuned starting in the bass, by pulling out the temperament strip one note at a time. This is continued until the top of the middle section has been reached. Then, the octaves in the top treble are checked before completing the tuning of the rest of the unisons.

It is a common mistake for tuners to play softly

as they tune the unisons. This may be because, when tuners are just learning, they soon find out that if they play a note hard while tuning unisons, it can de-tune the source note tuned previously.

It is easy, therefore, to get into the habit of tuning unisons softly. However, if the pins have been properly set during the temperament and octave stage, the danger of slippage is minimized.

A good habit to develop is to tune one side of the unison (always using the aforementioned "soft" blow), and then just before removing the strip loop and tuning the next note, quickly check the now pure unisons against the octave.

Unison Tuning in the Low Bass

The most commonly encountered problem in this area is a bichord that refuses to stop beating. First, check each string individually and listen carefully to see if it beats all by itself. This is relatively common in inexpensive pianos.

The cause of this is usually in the manufacturing process:

When the bass strings are installed, they need to have two or three half-twists in the direction of the winding. This not only keeps the winding tight on the core, but also prevents the string from being unwound during the stringing process.

To explain why this happens, you need to know how bass strings are made.

Traditionally, a string is made by stretching a core wire onto a device remarkably similar to a wood lathe. The core is looped at one end, and the loop is put on a hook attached to a bearing called a "Freewheel".

The other end of the core wire is then clamped into a vise at the other end of the lathe, and stretched to about 200 pounds per square inch.

A small anvil is then placed under the string, and the string is slightly flattened at the points where the winding starts and stops.

The core is then turned at a slow speed by a motor, and the winding is guided under tension onto the core by hand.

When the winding on has been completed, the ends of the winding are molded closed by "Swedging": An anvil with a special groove is placed under the ends, and a hammer is used to pound the ends of the windings together.

When the newly made string is released from the pressure of the lathe, the winding causes the string to coil slightly. The act of putting the string back under pressure in the piano, straightens the string, and that slight coil is transferred into a twisting motion to the core. Therefore, the string has to be twisted at least a little to actually make it straight.

An additional twist is given to the string to ensure that the winding does not loosen, and one more twist increases the volume of the partials by interfering with the way the string vibrates.

Make sure that the string has these two or three half-twists in the direction of the winding. If you are unsure about which direction the twist is to be made, look at the end of the string with a magnifying glass. The end of the winding literally points in the same direction as the twist to be made.

It is the string-maker's job to make sure beforehand that the core has no kinks, nicks or bends, and that the freewheel on the string lathe turns smoothly under pressure.

Modern string-making machines are powered on both ends of the lathe, so, theoretically, if the core is twisted before winding, it is purely the fault of the person installing the core on the lathe. If this is the cause of a false beat in a single wound string, the only solution is to replace it.

If the false beat is very slight, it is sometimes possible to cancel out the false beat by putting a small beat in the unisons in the opposite direction. This involves very carefully "playing" with the tuning of the two strings (i.e. muting the bad string, tuning the good string to the octave, and then tuning the bad string a little sharp or flat of the unison). Sometimes this works, sometimes it doesn't.

It is always best to have a new string made if a string has such a poor sound that it is difficult to tune, and ideally, bi-chords should be remade as a set.

To do this, measure the diameter of the core and the winding, then measure the distance in millimetres from the inside end of the anchor loop, to the start of the winding, and then the length of the winding. A string maker can use these four measurements to make a new string. Many string-makers ask for the note and string number, as well.

Before you rip the string out of the piano, however, make sure that the cause of the false beat isn't because of improper seating on the bridge.

Lightly tap the string into the crotch of the bridge pins with the end of a hammer shank. You can also tap the string very lightly down onto the bridge cap, as well, but make sure that you don't bury the string into the wood.

Unison Tuning in the High Treble

The plain wire strings in the treble often have false beats. This is because it only takes a very small amount of distress in the higher strings to affect their vibrating characteristics. A small bend, nick or twist in the wire can easily cause a false beat.

The most common fault is the string not seating properly on the bridge or the agraffe/nut. The next most common problem is the string receiving a bend as it passes around the bridge pin while flat. Then, when the string is pulled up to pitch, this bend becomes part of the speaking length. To correct this, use the end of a hammer shank to rub the bend out while the string is slightly sharp.

Another problem is the string being twisted during stringing. The only way to check if this is a problem is to loosen the string, pull the coil off the pin, and see if it twists. If it rotates a half a turn or more, then replace the string with a new one. If it stays straight or rotates only slightly, then the string is not twisted. However, it could be brittle or bent, so a replacement is probably a good idea.

One last possibility for false beats in plain wire is poor metal in the string. If the string is noticeably a different color than the rest, or if it is rusty, it should be replaced. If the tine breaks off the becket when removing the string, it is a sure sign that the string is brittle.

Often, time and budget restraints dictate how much tuning-related repair can be done. If it is the case that the above faults exist in the piano but a repair cannot be made, then the tuner is left with no choice but to do the best job he or she can.

Pitch Raising and Lowering

Common sense tells us that the closer a piano is to being on pitch, the more stable the final tuning is going to be. Therefore, if a piano is very flat or sharp, the pitch must be centralized before it is tuned.

How off-pitch must it be before a "pre-tuning" is needed? There is no real hard and fast answer. The better a piano is built and designed, the more stable it will be. Therefore, the point at which it is too far off-pitch is very different for pianos of different qualities.

Using a temperament strip to mute all unisons gives a very good indication when a piano MUST be pitch raised: If the muted unisons are so off-pitch as to be heard when played, then a pitch raise must be done. However, the shorter strings in the high treble mute so well, that you might not notice if it is just that section that is out.

If the bass section is badly out, but the top section is fine, raising the pitch in the bass could affect the tuning in the top end.

If the treble is quite flat or sharp, neglecting to stabilize the pitch first will almost certainly mean that fine-tuning will be a waste of time. Therefore, if there is any doubt, it is safer to pitch raise.

The Pitch Raise

The first step is to ascertain how flat the piano is.

Use your pitch fork to tune either middle C or the A above. Next, play all the C's or A's against the note you tuned, and find the flattest section. Tune the octave above your reference note sharp, so that it beats against the reference note at the same rate as against the flattest note. This note will now be half as sharp as the piano is flat.

NOTE: There is a limit to how far you can raise the pitch of the piano. An increase of 50 cents adds an incremental amount more in stress than the same amount at a lower pitch. I try to raise the pitch no more than 25 cents sharp of concert-pitch.

The object of setting the sharp pitch is not to "counteract" the flatness, but to compensate for how much the pitch will drop during the pitch raise.

For example: If you pitch-raised a piano that was 50 cents flat, up to concert pitch, by the time the tuning was done it will drop about 20 cents. If you pull the same piano up 75 cents to 25 cents sharp, by the time you finished, the piano will be close to concert-pitch or sharper by 5 or so cents.

If the same piano was 200 cents flat, pulling up the pitch 300 cents may leave the piano too sharp, or damage the piano in the process. With experience, you soon begin to sense what is too big a raise for the piano.

To be on the safe side, try not to raise the pitch more than 25 cents sharp in one pass.

Better-quality pianos may need much less of a raise above concert-pitch to make them stable. If you are in doubt, raise the pitch just a little above and be prepared to make two passes.

Strip all the unisons, except the top treble sections in an upright. Set a very rough and quick temperament to the concert-pitch note you tuned with you fork. Use this temperament to pull up the wound strings to concert-pitch. Leave the strip in the bass.

NOTE: **Wound strings should never be pulled up sharp as this can cause the winding to separate from the core, resulting in a buzzing string.**

Next, tune a new temperament as quickly as possible to the note you tuned sharp of concert-pitch.

You want it to be reasonably accurate, but you needn't spend a lot of energy on it: The pitch raise will destroy any hard work you put into it. (Plus, in order for a pitch raise to be effective and cost-efficient, it must be done quickly.)

It is important to note that in a pitch raise, time is of the essence. Don't worry too much about setting the pin; just make sure that the pin moves in the block enough to bring it slightly above pitch. When you release tension on the pin, the note should fall down close to the desired pitch.

Next, pull up the middle strings of the middle section using octaves off the temperament. In a grand piano, you can continue into the treble sections, but instead of tuning to an octave, tune to a perfect fifth up until you reach an octave above the middle section.

Tuning to the fifth will make the treble section increasingly sharp.

This is important, because as you raise the pitch of the rest of the piano, the treble will flatten more due to the added stress than will the rest. After you have tuned up to an octave above the middle, you can go back to the bass and pull out the temperament strip, tuning the unisons until you reach the point in the treble where you left off. Finally, tune the remaining treble strings to the octave below.

NOTE: If the piano is VERY flat, perhaps due to stringing or Tuning Pin Resetting, you may want to consider tuning a rough temperament and then tuning each note an octave at a time in order to spread the stress across the piano.

In very cheap uprights, the stress of a big pitch raise can, in rare instances, cause the plate to break.

I have seen this happen to other tuners three times during the last forty-odd years. Two of those times, it was a Lesage upright built in the early sixties.

To avoid this possibility, tune the temperament, and then all of the "F's" down in the bass, and then all the "F's" up into the treble, then all the "F#'s", "G's", etc.

In an upright piano, because the top treble is not stripped, you can, while you are learning, use either a rubber mute or a Papp's mute.

It is important, though, that you use the mute so that you are tuning the strings in order, and not using the Papp's mute to tune the centre strings first. This is done only while touching up a drifted octave, not while tuning or pitch raising.

Ideally, however, there is a much faster way to pitch raise in the treble, but it does take practice and concentration: Muteless Tuning.

Muteless Tuning

The three strings in the unison can be individually raised 25 cents or more without mutes. This not only is a great timesaver, but it also can be fun because of the challenge involved.

Basically, the principle behind it is this: Normally when we tune, we listen to the sound of beating between two notes. In muteless tuning, we ignore the beats, and instead, listen to the sound of an individual string moving up in pitch. We can estimate roughly the pitch of the note when we hear it slide up until it stops moving. At that point, because we have brought it above pitch, it is so different from the other notes that it stands out.

First, play the octave below the note that is to be tuned, and remember that pitch. Starting with the left-hand unison in the note to be tuned, pull it up in pitch while playing the note repeatedly. Stop raising the pitch when it reaches the point that it seems a little sharper than the reference note we played first.

Next, raise the middle string of the unison until it sounds pure with the first string. In order to hear this, you have to ignore the sound of the right-hand string, and listen instead to the sound of the string coming up to "meet" the left-hand string.

If you are unsure at first, either pluck the strings to hear their pitch individually, or use your mute. With practice, you will soon be able to hear all three strings at the same time and guess fairly accurately what their pitch is in relation to your reference note, and to each other.

You have three goals to meet during the pitch raise: Speed; a sharp treble; and pulling up the bass only up to pitch. Your eventual goal is to leave the piano on-pitch or slightly above.

Pitch Lowering

The two most commons reasons to lower the pitch of a piano are: Correction of an overshot pitch raise, and correction of the effect of an extreme raise in humidity since the last tuning.

Normally, an overzealous pitch raise results in high pitch just in the top treble. However, if the pitch raise is started too high, it can affect the whole piano (but hopefully not the wound strings).

An increase of pitch due to high humidity is normally not as extreme, and is generalized across the instrument. Sometimes, an increase in humidity can result in an especial sharpness in the tenor strings just above the section break, or the top treble.

Generally speaking, the pitch of each section is lowered just as a normal tuning would be accomplished. Although, if the pitch of the top treble is extremely high, it would be wise to stop at the top and work down so that you don't put undue stress on the highest strings as you reduce the tension of the lower strings.

Feel the pin turn in the block as you lower the pitch slightly below where you want it. Hopefully, when you release the tension of your tuning hammer from the pin, the note should rise up to the desired pitch.

Once again, the goal is speed rather than accuracy, and leaving the piano at a pitch centre where fine-tuning will be stable.

It is impossible to tune a piano perfectly. Even if you have done the best job imaginable, the tuning will drift because of environmental reasons and there is nothing you can do about it.

All that conscientious tuners can do, is to do the

best job they can, in the situation they are given. To obsess about perfection in a situation where perfection is fleeting, is futile.

The Art of Compromise lies in a tuner's ability to take an imperfect instrument and make it the best it can be.

Additional Exercises

In order to tune quickly and accurately, every piano tuner should spend some time practicing the three subjects covered in this section: Keyboard Technique, Ear Training, and Speed/Accuracy Drills. They are all related, and one way or another, practicing one will improve the others.

I also believe that it is a good idea that the tuner who doesn't play the piano should learn at least one song to play after the job is finished. The customer expects it, and it is like the exclamation mark at the end of a sentence!

The whole tuning experience for the technician becomes a journey with a goal.

I promise you that in a relatively short period of time, you will play your one piece with the panache of a pro.

My brother, John, an excellent guitarist and

piano tuner, taught himself to play Beethoven's "Für Elise", and now that he has been playing it everyday for years, plays it better than any pro on record.

I would encourage you to practice these exercises diligently. Having taught music for over forty years, I know that the worst students are often the adults. However, their excuse is always "I couldn't find the time to practice." The tuner has no such excuse. Every day, you play the piano as a trade; every day, you are practicing.

Many of these exercises can be fit into your tuning as part of the job. The customer will probably not notice, and you won't even notice how hard you have actually worked on them. All you will see is how much you have improved and how fast it has happened.

Keyboard Technique

Music is a language, just like English, French or Chinese.

Think for a moment how you learned to speak your mother tongue.

The very first step was hearing the people around you speak.

The second step was learning to understand

some of these sounds you heard and making similar noises.

The third step was making the same noises in the same order and inflection, and understanding what you say, and what you hear, as well.

The fourth step was a long period of increasing how many words you knew to the point where the spoken language is simply a part of who you are.

The fifth step was learning how to read and write. The sixth step was learning how to express your thoughts in written form, so that no matter who read it, they would know something about you and what you were thinking.

You can be just as fluent in music as you are in language. All it takes is patience, and the willingness to make the effort that each step requires.

Music as a Second Language

Here are the previously mentioned stages of fluency broken down into a list, and related directly towards learning music as a second language:

The Listening Stage

An infant needs the first two years of life to pass through this first stage because of their developing brain. For an adult, it is a much shorter period.

Studies done in total immersion language teaching have shown that most people need between four to six weeks of exposure to another language for the sound and syntax of the language to be absorbed by the adult mind.

Luckily, you don't have to go to another country to experience music. Music is more prevalent in western culture than most people even realize. Not only is it a form of entertainment, but it has also become the background to our daily lives. From elevators to movies, we are constantly exposed to the language of music. However, many of us ignore it. We "tune" it out.

As music students, we can make a conscious effort to listen to the music around us, and become aware of the sound and syntax of the musical language.

One way to define music is to say that it is pitch and rhythm organized in time.

The untrained musical ear is attuned to the concept of "Melody" – the tune you sing along to - but music is much more than that.

When you listen to music, you should try to listen for all the other aspects of the whole – other instruments, other voices, the rhythm, and the form.

The form of music is one of the best keys to understanding a piece of music.

Think of the form of music like the structure of a story. Every story is made up of many things, and being literate, we can easily break it down into the smallest parts: Letters make words, words make sentences, and sentences make paragraphs. Every sentence contains a subject and a predicate: i.e. John likes ice cream. John is the subject, and what he likes is the predicate.

Every paragraph contains a complete thought. When we speak, read or write, we rarely think about all these details; however, they still exist, and that is what makes a language.

In every piece of music there are notes. Notes make up sequences, sequences make phrases, and phrases make up melody. The notes have other notes along with them to make chords. They have a rhythm to them just like speech. Finally, all the notes, chords, sequences, and phrases have a structure that organizes them together and makes them logical to the listener.

They are usually organized into sections that can be identified as being unique or repeated – they have a beginning, middle, and an end. Best of all, as far as understanding them goes, they are often accompanied by words, and organized into genre.

The form of a pop song, for instance, can be easily broken down into sections, and the instrumentation and rhythm are recognizable to the untrained ear. Music of other genres, and even cultures, can be broken down and analyzed in the same way, but sometimes, it takes a little more training.

Take the time to really listen to the music around you, and start thinking about what you are hearing in terms of these concepts. Listen to what the drummer is doing, or the bass player, or any other part of the song other than the melody.

Believe it or not, the only difference between a musician and a non-musician (in the pop music world, at least), is that musicians listen, and try to understand what is happening in the song they are listening to.

Even the most amateurish songwriter knows that every song has a form, and instrumentation, and a rhythm. They have taken the time to go through the steps and gain at least some form of fluency in the language of music.

The Noisemaking Stage

Besides being a cute sound to the parents, or a cry of hunger, babies make noise because they are experimenting with the sounds they can make themselves. They play with these noises until they begin to form sounds recognizable as language.

The fact of the matter is that this is actually fun for infants. They love to hear the sound of their own voice. (Some never grow out of this stage.)

This stage in learning music can be fun, as well. No baby is ever embarrassed about going through the ga-ga-go-goo stage. Neither should we. Luckily, we can be alone while we do it.

When an infant vocalizes, two distinct things are happening: They are exercising their vocal chords, preparing them to make the right sounds, and they are learning how to control these sounds.

This second stage for a beginning pianist is fairly simple, but important. What you have to do is prepare your fingers to work in the right way to make music.

This is how it's done:

Sit up straight at the keyboard at a height so that when your fingers are on the keys, your forearms are parallel to the floor.

Put each of your fingers on a key so that each hand has five fingers on five keys comfortably.

The keys are played by the fingertips only. Your knuckles should be curled, and the backs of your hands in line with your forearms. (Piano teachers have been known to tape rulers across the forearm, wrist, and the back of the hand to ensure that this rule is not broken.)

When you play the keys, use the weight of your arms. **Do not lift your fingers off the keys!** Raise your knuckles, **(don't raise your wrist!)**, straighten your fingers slightly, and let the weight of your arms play the keys. Your fingers and wrists have to be relaxed, and act like little shock-absorbers as the weight of your arms bring them downwards.

Practice this motion until it is second nature. Relaxed and tensionless, your hands merely position your fingers – the arms do all the work.

When the mechanics of this exercise are firmly ingrained into your hands and mind, practice doing the same thing on a different set of keys, then changing sets each time. Think about your posture, your hand and arm position, and most of all, think about keeping tension out of your hands and wrists.

The next exercise is to do exactly the same process, but this time lifting your hands six inches into the air, and bringing the fingers down on the keys you want, never letting any tense up, and using your fingers as shock-absorbers.

Spend fifteen minutes a day for two weeks doing this. Follow the rules, and above all – have fun making some noise! By the time you have finished this stage, your fingers will be one with the keys.

All that is needed to make music now, is "facility" - which musicians call "Technique".

The Imitation Stage

It is a very unfortunate fact that most piano teachers skip this stage. I believe that it is one of the main reasons why some students quit, and many others never learn to play by ear.

There are two steps to this stage: The first is acquiring technique, and the second is experimentation.

Although many students are scared off by the practice of technique, it is actually one of the best parts about music. Practicing technique can be a zen-like experience where your body goes into autopilot and your mind drifts off into someplace else entirely.

In order for this to happen, though, a commitment of time is needed. Like meditation, it will only be enjoyable and relaxing if you commit the time to it and forget everything else.

It doesn't have to be a big commitment of time. In fact, it could be five minutes, three times a day – but it has to be every day, preferably more than once a day, and probably for at least a month or two.

In the previous stage, you got used to having fingers on the keys, playing properly. Now, it's time to make the fingers work individually.

Each of the following points is one step. Be comfortable with each step before moving on.

Take the same sets of keys used earlier, and play them one at a time. It can be in any order, or no order at all; hands separately, or together. In the beginning, the only thing you have to think about is making sure that you don't tense up. If your hands are tense, stop playing and shake the tension lightly out.

Don't play until it hurts! Stop before it hurts, and get to know your limits. Better to spend five minutes or less several times a day, than one big block of time. Babies rarely goo for longer then a few minutes. After a few times, you'll notice that you can do this longer each time.

Try making some kind of order to the notes you are playing. It can be the pattern of notes, or the rhythm. The important thing is that you start to exercise some kind of control over your fingers in a logical and repeatable fashion.

Change your position on the keyboard. Use other notes. Incorporate small intervals and black notes.

The important thing about these initial stages is that they must be repeated over and over, stopping only when you become aware that you are tensing up, or about to get sore. Unlike weightlifting, the rule is "No Pain, Great Gain!"

Invent sequences of notes to practice that may sound familiar in some way. For instance: Five-note scales up and down, or "Doe, a deer a female deer. Ray, a drop of golden sun".

When I was a teenager, I taught myself how to play the five-string banjo by playing the fingerpicking patterns over and over while my Dad and I watched T.V.

It was a measure of my Dad's character that he never asked me to stop. All he would say is, "You're having trouble there. Slow down, son".

Therein lies the key to practicing anything, whether a sequence of notes or an entire piece: Play it slowly until you have mastered it at that speed, then speed up.

If you make a mistake, slow down so that you are a little faster than the speed you can do it at. If you have a metronome, the rule is: Two clicks ahead, and one click back.

Two steps forward and one step back will always get you where you are going if you have patience.

Practice sequences where your thumb crosses under your finger to play a note.

The technical secret to playing anything on the piano is fingering. The secret to fingering is that your thumb crosses under your fingers, or your fingers over your thumb. Fingers never cross over fingers.

Normally, the practice of technique is associated with playing scales. However, I think of scales as being part of the process of acquainting one's ear and technique with a specific key signature.

If you want to learn some scales, get a scale book and practice them with the right fingering. Don't try to fake it. There is really no point and it is probably counterproductive.

The important things in this stage are:

1. Regular practice.
2. Repetitive motions.
3. Proper posture and hand positions.
4. No Pain, Great Gain.
5. Experimenting with patterns and rhythms.

Now, for the Experimental part of the Imitation Stage: Your fingers are now accustomed to playing the keys, and your brain has some ability to control them.

Use this hard-won facility to try to play some of the music you know and hear. Think of a song and hum the melody. Find the notes you are humming on the keyboard, and practice getting them in the right order, then the right rhythm, then the right tempo. In doing this, you are training your fingers, your ear, and your mind.

Always remember: Proper posture and hand position, "No Pain, Great Gain", and "Two clicks forward, one click back".

The Speaking Stage

This stage is a long period of time invested into being able to play more pieces by ear. Not just the melody, but also the bass line of songs, the vocal harmonies, the chords used, and even the rhythm of the drums – either on the keyboard or tapped with your hand on your knees.

It is possible to go through this stage on your own, but it is faster and easier if you have some guidance. It is almost always possible to find a music teacher who will teach you in exchange for your tuning services. The key is to find someone you like, who can relate to you, and is willing to teach you to play by ear.

The ideal piano teacher has three qualities: They must be a musician, fluent in music, and not just a pianist. They must teach you music, not just piano, and they must be enthusiastic about what they do. If they love music, and love teaching, you'll probably love being taught music by them.

The Reading and Writing Stage

This also requires some guidance, although it is easier to teach yourself how to be musically literate than it would seem. In fact, this process is easier than the speaking stage, providing you actually went through that stage first.

Learning how to read and write music before learning how to play is like trying to teach someone to read and write a language before they can speak it. It makes no sense, and becomes an academic exercise rather than a practical skill.

In order for you to finish this chapter, you will need to know a little about reading music. These are very rudimentary lessons, enough for you to explore further exercises in tuning, but just scratching the surface.

In language terms, reading music goes from "See Dick, see Jane" to Shakespeare, to mathematical theorems. There is always more to learn, more complexities to grasp.

For the purposes of this book, we'll stick to "Dick and Jane". Music is written on paper in a way that it shows both pitch and rhythm. Remember, music is pitch and rhythm organized in time. It is a type of graph in a way. The X-axis shows the pitch, the Y-axis, the time.

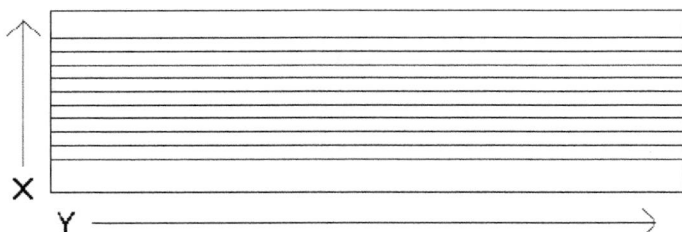

The higher up the X-axis a note is placed, the higher the pitch; the farther along the Y-axis, the further along in time. The number of lines in this graph represents specific keys on the keyboard. In order to make it easier to read, the graph is split apart at middle C.

Middle C itself is between these two split-apart sections. Whenever a C is to be written, you not only write the note in the middle, but you put in the missing line.

In order to further help you identify which note goes on what line, you add signs at the beginning of the graph, which are called "Clefs".

The graph that represents the keyboard above middle C gets a "Treble Clef" or "G Clef". It is called this because it is an old fashioned way of writing a capital G, and it literally curls around the line that represents the G above middle C. Any note written on this line, therefore, is a G.

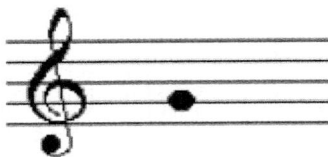

The graph that represents the notes on the keyboard below middle C has a sign at the beginning called a "Bass Clef" or an "F Clef". Once again, this sign is an old-fashioned stylized capital F. Instead of the two arms sticking out like our F, it has two dots. These dots are on either side of the line that represents the F below middle C. Therefore, any note put on this line will be that F.

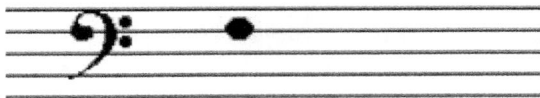

Put together, the two graphs or "Staffs" are called a "Stave", which looks like this:

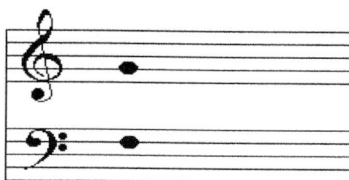

Now you know where on the stave is the F below middle C, middle C itself, and the G above, but what are the other lines? Well, the lines each represent a note, but so do the spaces between them. Here's an easy way to remember which lines represent which note:

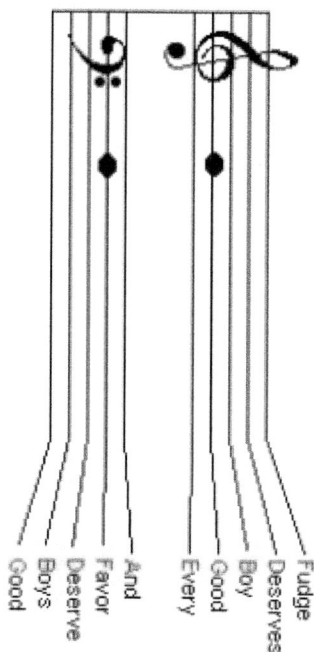

As you can see, the lines represent from the bottom up: G, B, D, F, and A below middle C, and E, G, B, D, and F above middle C. In between those lines are the rest of the notes.

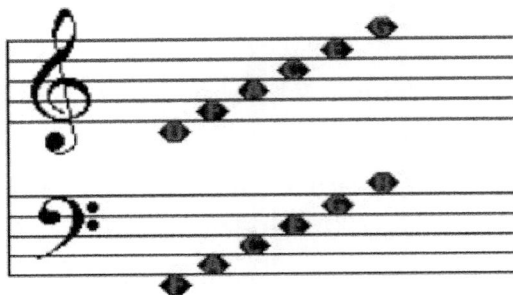

Now you know the rudiments of how pitch is written down. Using what you have just learned, we can take the Temperament Pattern #1 "Chasing the Tail" and write it down as notes.

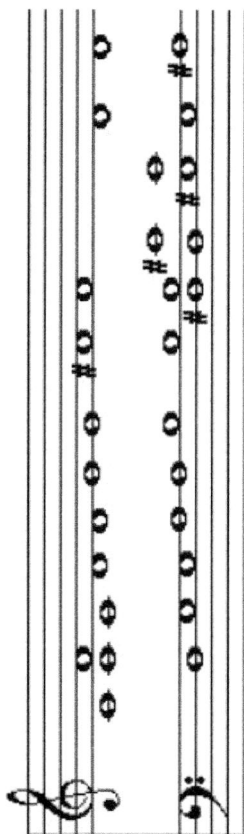

The Whole Note. The whole note gets four beats. It's called a whole note because in the time signature of 4/4 or "Common Time", four beats is the entire, or whole, measure.

The Half Note. The half note gets two beats, or "half" of a measure.

The Quarter Note. The quarter note gets one beat, or a quarter of a four beat measure.

The Eighth Note. The eighth note gets a half of a beat, or one-eighth of a measure.

Any of these notes can be increased in length by half of its value by adding a little dot after the note. Therefore, a "dotted" half note gets three beats instead of two.

If, at the beginning of a stave, we see the time signature 4/4 or a "C" (for common time), we note that there is four beats to a measure, and a quarter note (the bottom four of the time signature) gets one beat.

The following example shows four measures in common time. Each measure has the right amount of notes adding up to four beats; however, apart from the first two bars, a little simple math is needed to prove that statement true.

The easy way to figure out the rhythm of the notes is to count the beats. To count the eighth notes, which get half a beat, we say "and".

I can write out the same rhythm with words. Just say the following at an even beat:

One and two and three and four and, **one** and **two** and **three** and **four** and, **one** and two and **three** and **four and, one** and two **and three and** four **and**.

Just say the bold words louder than the rest, and you hear the rhythm notated below.

Notice that I wrote out "and", even when there are no eighth notes in the measure. Saying: "One and Two and" will help you keep the beats and notes in the right places.

So, now you know how pitch and rhythm are notated. Play the following example: Remember, anything is easy if you break it down into smaller bits.

Figure out the pitch of the notes, then which fingers play them, then the rhythm, then put it all together starting slowly, and getting faster.

Hopefully, you will recognize this tune. (I may have to write a different example for the international versions of this book!)

Remember the way your hands were positioned on the keys in the early noisemaking stage of learning. Each finger has a key, but if you HAVE to cross over, fingers over the thumb, or thumb under the fingers!

When there is a full stave (two staffs), the upper staff (the treble) is played by the right hand. The bottom staff (the bass) is played by the left hand. Here is the end of the above piece, but played with the left hand:

In most simple pieces of music, the left hand plays a bass line, and sometimes some harmony. Here are the first four bars again, but this time with a full stave, melody, bass (and harmony):

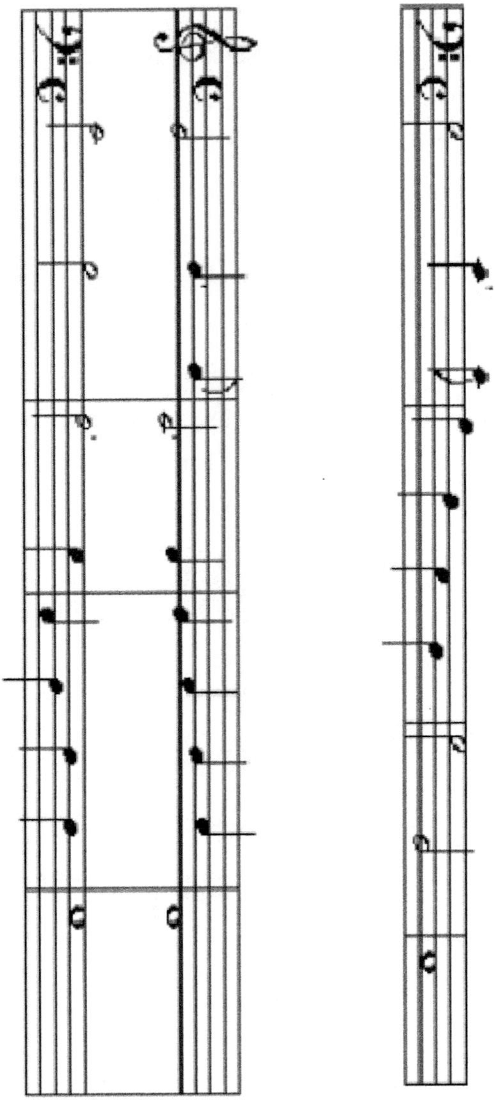

There are hundreds of books available for easy piano. If you would like more examples, pick up a few to practice with.

An alternative to buying easy piano books is to use a hymnbook. Everything you need to know about keyboard playing, theory, harmony and form is contained in a single hymnbook.

I literally taught myself how to play the piano and read music by starting at the beginning of the United Church's Red Hymn book, playing each vocal part separately, then together, and pushing myself through to the end. By the time I had finished, I could sight read anything, understood harmony and notation, and played piano well enough to enter the music program at the University of Calgary. The entire process from beginning to end only took me less than two years!

The Expression Stage

This is the final stage of fluency. Once you have a good grasp of the language of music, you can compose your own.

I know that many of us think up catchy tunes, but if you can't write them down, they are just folk-songs to be passed along (or kept to oneself.)

For a poet to be a poet, an author to be an author, or a composer to be a composer, they have to be able to write their compositions down. This stage, like its corollary in language, is best learned from a qualified teacher.

Keyboard Training Exercises

In order to smoothly test consecutive intervals, practice the following exercises until you can perform them quickly and effortlessly. Make sure you follow the directions exactly and use the proper fingering!

Chromatic Scales

Playing each semitone in a row, up or down, is referred to as a chromatic scale. The proper hand position is essential in order to play the scale quickly. In order to see this position and "get the feel" of it, Take your right hand and place your fingers on a table in the proper hand position for playing. Put the thumb, first, and second finger side by side and slightly lift your ring finger and little finger off the table. Now move your elbow slightly off to the right.

Take that same hand position and move it onto the keyboard so that your thumb finger is on middle C, and your middle finger is on C#.

Now, take your left hand and place your fingers on a table just like you did for your right hand. Put the thumb, first, and index finger side by side and slightly lift your ring finger and little finger off the table. Now move your elbow slightly off to the left.

Take that same hand position and move it onto the keyboard so that your middle finger is on middle C, and your thumb is on B.

From C going up, this is the fingering for the chromatic scale: Thumb, middle, thumb, middle, thumb, index, middle, thumb, middle, thumb, middle, thumb, etc. The only keys the index finger plays are the F's and the C's.

From top C going down, this is the right-hand fingering for the chromatic scale: Middle, thumb, middle, thumb, middle, thumb, middle, index, thumb, middle, thumb, middle, index, etc.

NOTE: As a general rule, all scales are played so that the thumb only plays white keys, and never the black keys.

To play a chromatic scale going down with your left hand, start on middle C with your thumb, then index, middle, thumb, middle, thumb, middle, thumb, index, middle, thumb, middle, etc.

It's the same pattern as going up, but in reverse. Notice that the two hands have the same fingering.

Start slowly, and only speed up as you gain proficiency. "Two clicks up, one click back."

Chromatic Scales in Octaves

Now practice the chromatic scales with both hands together. Notice that when the right hand's thumb is playing a key, the left hand's thumb is doing the same.

Be very diligent with practicing this scale. Start very slowly, preferably using a metronome. When you have a speed mastered, then speed up two clicks. Go back one click if you make a mistake. Practice until you can play this scale with both hands as fast as you can with one.

Various Parallel Intervals

Using a metronome, practice doing scales of the various tuning intervals: Twelfths, tenths, sixths, fifths, fourths and thirds. Make sure you use the proper fingering in each hand as learned in the previous exercises.

This is a little trickier because the thumbs and fingers are no longer doing the same thing at the same time. Use the metronome, and increase your speed slowly.

Ear Training

Learning to tune in itself is ear training. However, just hearing beats is not all that the professional tuner needs to be able to do.

In this chapter, you will find exercises designed to help you refine your listening skills, and help you to understand what it is you are actually hearing.

The following is a list of all the individual aspects of a tuning that the tuner must recognize and understand. For each item, I have included an exercise. Practice these while you are learning, and again after you have been tuning for a short period of time.

Not only will they help students learning to tune, but they will also help refine the skills of the professional tuner, and serving as a guide to how far you have progressed.

Perfect Pitch

I have been asked many times over the years if I must have "Perfect Pitch" to tune a piano. Of course, the answer is no. However, the very fact that they asked the question in the first place proves that they don't understand the concept of "Perfect Pitch".

The perfect pitch that most people are familiar with is the ability to identify the pitch of a note without a reference. Often this means not only if a note is a C or an F#, but also if it is "In Tune". In many ways, this ability is nothing more than a kind of parlour trick. It is impressive to those who can't do it, and especially impressive to those who wish they could.

For most people, the ability to identify notes out of thin air is a hard-won learned skill. But, for a lucky few, it is a talent that seemed to develop overnight.

Once again, it is like language. In a sample population, there are always people who have a natural ability with language, either as a writer, or as a public speaker. Sometimes these abilities seem effortless, but the truth is that even the talented have to work at honing their skills.

The secret is that the real talent lies in having such a great interest in the subject, that even the studying and hard work involved in mastering the skill is enjoyable - even exciting.

There are different types of "Perfect Pitch". The most common among musicians is called "Acquired Relative Pitch". This is the skill, learned through experience and practice, of being able to identify any pitch by using one starting pitch, and finding any other by using a reference.

For instance, a singer should be able to look at a piece of written music and sing what is written by just knowing the key of the music and being given a starting pitch. When you think of it, this is not such a difficult task. Most of us can sing a song we know without music. A musician is simply reading what is written and singing just as if it were a story read out loud.

Having Acquired Relative Pitch also means, that if you gave a singer a C, and told them to sing an F#, they could do it. This is simply a learned skill. All you need is the ability to sing in key – if you play a note on the piano, you can sing the same note.

The next most common kind of perfect pitch is called "Perfect Acquired Relative Pitch". This is merely one more refinement in musical skill. It is the ability to discern the pitch of any given note, without a reference.

For instance, being able to tell what pitch a note is without finding it on an instrument. Many instrumentalists develop this skill through repetition. Violinists can often sing an "A" if asked, because every day they tune their instruments using an "A". Trumpet players can sing a Bb, French Horn players, an F. They "learn" the sound of a pitch merely through endless repetition.

Professional guitarists can often sing an "E" on cue, and they also have the learned ability to be able to tell what specific chord another guitarist is using because they recognize the specific combination of notes in that chord.

Jazz players call this "Voicing". There are many ways to play each chord, and all those different ways are different voicings of that chord. This isn't an innate talent – it is the product of years of practicing.

Acquired Perfect Pitch is not as common as the previous instances. However, it is still quite common among the best musicians. Some musicians' ears are so well trained, that they can tell a difference in pitch, without a reference, in terms of cycles per second. They can literally hear the tempering in notes – the difference in pitch of a tempered and non-tempered note – even when both notes are in tune in their own context.

I knew a musician who, when given a random recording of a concert piece, could not only tell you the name and composer of the piece, but he could also tell you if the piano, or the recording, was sharp or flat of concert-pitch; what kind of piano it was; who was playing it; and when it was recorded. This is not a gift. It is the natural by-product of intensive study, endless enthusiasm, and the lack of a normal social life.

Some people with acquired perfect pitch say that they "see" pitch in terms of colour. They have learned to associate the key of a piece of music with a certain hue. F is dark blue, G is green, etc.

True Innate Perfect Pitch is immeasurably rare, and in many ways it is a curse rather than a gift. Having true perfect pitch means that hearing a note, or a combination of notes, that is not perfectly in tune with one another mathematically, is actually painful.

A piano tuner with a keenly trained ear may be annoyed by the sound of an un-tuned piano, but that is only because he can fix the problem. With true perfect pitch, even a well-tuned piano is annoying because it is tempered. These people never become musicians. In fact, they avoid listening to music at all. They have the most in common with people of a slightly less rare disability, Monotonalism.

True monotones lack the ability to either process pitch out of a certain narrow range, or to physically reproduce a normal range of speaking pitches.

Most monotones literally speak monotonally or can't speak at all. Some monotones are classified as deaf, because they can only hear in such a small tonal range.

The classic cop-out of "Oh, I can't sing! I'm tone-deaf" is the ultimate misuse of terminology. If that statement were true, they wouldn't even have to say it. They couldn't hear the question, couldn't speak the answer, or simply would not have been asked. A speaking tone-deaf person is instantly recognizable. All of the normal inflections in speech are absent or severely limited.

When someone says that they are "Tone-Deaf", it usually means that they have never actually listened to the sound of their own voice when they sing. In most cases, an off-key singer can be taught to sing on-key by teaching them how to listen - not only to what they are singing, but how it relates to what they are singing to.

When people ask me if I have perfect pitch, I tell them (with a smile) that I have Qualified Imperfect Acquired Relative Pitch, or "Quiarp". Given enough time and enough hints, I can usually make a close guess as to the pitch of a note – as long as I don't have to be right all the time.

On an average day, the lowest note I can sing comfortably is a D two octaves below middle C, and the highest I can sing is a D an octave above. To identify a note, I'll sing my highest or lowest note and then estimate the interval between my note and the given note.

Sometimes this works, and sometimes it doesn't. What's important is that I can tell if a piano is in tune or not.

Pitch

Exercise #1

Find out for yourself what your vocal range is and practice the somewhat less-than-astounding parlour trick of "Quiarp". Sing your lowest note and your highest note, and find out which notes they are on the piano. Check it out every time you pass a piano keyboard over a few days to make sure that you know what your range actually is. Once you're sure, then do the opposite; sing the two notes and then play the keys. If you do this often enough, you will eventually be able to match those two notes very closely, almost every time.

Exercise #2

I call this the "Bathroom Break Test". The next time you are tuning and have to stop in the middle to visit the washroom, sing softly to yourself the last note you tuned. While you are away from the piano, hum this note every once and a while to yourself. When you return, test to see if you are still humming the same pitch. If you're not, start by almost constantly humming that one note. If you are on pitch, increase the amount of the challenge, i.e. Only hum when you leave and when you return, or hum the next note to be tuned after playing the note before, etc.

Exercise #3

Carry one of your tuning forks with you wherever you go. If you normally use an "A: 440" fork, then carry the "C: 523.3", etc.

Listen to the pitch of the fork as often as you can. Hum or whistle the pitch as you listen. After doing this for a few days, hum or whistle before you play the fork, and see how close you can guess the pitch. Some musicians have told me that this was how they acquired "Perfect Pitch".

The Individual Pitch of One String

Exercise #1

Every once and a while, when you are tuning unisons, pluck the three strings individually and try to identify which string is sharp or flat without playing a reference note. Then, tune the first unison to the reference, pluck the others and try to identify in what way they relate to the now-tuned unison.

Are the others sharp or flat, and by how much?

Tune the remaining unisons by plucking only – muting the other strings each time you pluck. By plucking the strings in this manner, your ability to hear the beats is removed, so you are forced to tune by listening only to their relative pitch. (Make sure to test the setting of the pin before moving on.)

Exercise #2

When doing a big pitch raise in a piano, have a C.D. of music playing in the background – preferably piano music. Play the piece on repeat, find the most dominant note repeated in the piece on another tuned piano or keyboard, and then tune all the keys on the piano that match the note in the piece.

When all the "C's" are tuned, skip to the next track and find a different note. This exercise is a preliminary to an advanced exercise described later in this chapter.

The Sound of Two Strings
Interacting with One Another

Exercise # 1

When tuning a piano that is basically on pitch but with poor unisons, lay in a good temperament, and then strip the remainder of the piano so the strip only mutes every other unison. (i.e. The left string on one note, and the right string of the note above.)

Play your reference note, and tune the octave without muting the other unison. Listen to how the string moves initially.

Do the beats in the unisons get faster or slower? What do the beats between the octave and the two unisons do?

Try to estimate how much and in which way to tune the string in order to get it closer to the octave. Tune the other unison to see if your estimation was correct.

After this has been done a number of times, you should start to hear how the relationship between the two out-of-tune unisons relates to the tuned reference note.

Exercise #2

Prepare the piano as in Exercise #1. Play your reference note, and then tune the unisons by remembering the pitch of the reference. Play the reference as much as you need, but do not play it at the same time as the note you are tuning.

This is a good exercise to prepare you for Muteless Tuning.

The Sound of Three Strings
Interacting with Each Other

Exercises #1 & #2

Repeat the two exercises above without the temperament strip. Use a piano that is severely flat when starting to do these exercises.

Exercise #3

When setting the temperament, tune an octave above the last tuned note, and play both notes while tuning the next interval.

This will work if you have a feel for how narrow or wide you are making the note without having to hear the beats exactly.

The Sound of a Semitone

Exercise #1

I am told that this exercise is commonly given as a test to new or visiting tuners to the Steinway Factory.

Strip the temperament, and tune your starting note and the octave above to your fork. Next, tune each semitone between the two reference notes a semitone at a time. C, C#, D, D#, etc. - without any checks.

When you reach the reference note at the top, see how close or far away your last tuned note is to the reference in comparison to the other semitones.

Most tuners have a tendency to make a semitone too large, making the last note obviously sharp of the top reference.

Start at the beginning again and make each semitone closer together until you manage to end up with a fairly close approximation of semitones from the top to the bottom.

Finally, tune the temperament as you normally would, and pay attention to how far off your last semitone-by-semitone attempt was.

The Sound of the Intervals

As piano tuners, we normally listen for the beats between strings. It is important, however, that we learn the sound of the intervals, and can recognize which intervals are which just by their sound. When pitch raising in fifths, for instance, if we can't recognize a fifth, it makes it almost impossible to bring a severely flat string up into a fifth.

Exercise #1

On a tuned piano, play each of the intervals and try to recognize their sound no matter where on the keyboard.

At first, try very hard to make sure that you have the right interval before you play it.

For instance, if you are going to play a fifth with

the right hand, place your thumb on a note without playing it. Count eight keys up from that note (including the note under your thumb), put your little finger on the eighth note, and then play the interval. Major Third = 5 notes, Perfect Fourth = 6 notes, Major Sixth = 10.

Exercise #2

On a tuned piano, have someone else play the intervals, and without looking, try to figure out what interval it is. It is preferable to do this with someone who knows the intervals themselves.

Exercise #3

Challenge yourself to try to sing the intervals before hearing it. For instance, play a "C", and then try to sing the P5 "G" above, then play the G and see if you're right.

The Sound of Compound Intervals

A compound interval is an interval with more than an octave difference. For instance, a Major third plus an octave is called a "Tenth".

This interval is especially handy when tuning in the lower register. Just as Major thirds slow down as they get lower, the tenths do the same thing.

As large intervals are easier to hear in the bass, the tenth is often used to check the tuning of the octaves in the bass.

The most commonly used compound intervals are the Tenth, the Twelfth (Fifth + Octave), the Fifteenth (Double Octave), and the Nineteenth (Fifth + two Octaves).

Do the three previous exercises with compound intervals. (For Exercise #3, use a lower starting note so you don't hurt yourself!)

The Sound of an Octave

Although this one may seem like a no-brainer, there are two interesting exercises that you can perform if you are comfortable with singing.

Exercise #1

Play a note, sing that note, then stop and sing the octave above. Not only is this good training for singing, but it helps exercise your brain's ability to "visualize" a note.

Exercise #2

Play a note, and then sing the octave above while still holding the note. Purposefully, but slowly, slide the note you are singing slightly sharp, then slightly flat, then on-pitch. Do this with as many different notes as you are comfortable singing.

The Sound of an Octave Stretch

When you are tuning, try this little exercise to check the difference between Perfect and Stretched Octaves:

Exercise #1

After setting the temperament with your "A" fork, tune, in Perfect octaves, all the other A's. When you get to the point that you are tuning those notes during your normal octave tuning, check and see if they are flat according to your temperament.

Exercise #2

If you get the opportunity, tune two similar pianos in similar rooms so that one has a blended nonstretch tuning, and the other has a normal stretch tuning. Have someone play the pianos, stand back, and listen to the difference in the sound. (Better yet, have someone else do the tunings while you fix yourself a drink.)

Speed Drills

Exercise #1

Carry a stopwatch with you when you tune. Check how long it takes you to tune each step: How long for the temperament, the octaves, the unisons, etc. Calculate your average time over ten pianos, and then each subsequent time, challenge yourself to be a little faster.

Exercise #2

Buy a small hourglass-type egg timer and use Cyanoacrylatic (Krazy) Glue to securely fasten the stand on each end. Turn the timer every time you move to a new string.

If you consistently beat the timer every time, carefully drill a tiny hole through one of the bases and let out a little sand. Close the hole with tape, and use the timer again to time how long it takes for you (on average) to tune each string.

Keep letting out a little sand until you reach the point that you have to force yourself to speed up in order to keep up with the timer. If you reach the point where you consistently beat the timer once more, let out some more sand.

NOTE: Most tuners are capable of more speed than they realize. They re-tune notes that are already in tune, they use too many checks, and generally waste time. Trying to "Beat the Clock" will help you see how efficient your skills really are.

Exercise #3

Before you start a tuning, make an educated guess as to how long the tuning will take, based on the quality of the piano and the state of the tuning. After you have finished, check and see how accurate your guess was. Do this enough times so that your guesses become more accurate.

Most tuners underestimate (sometimes wildly) how long their tunings take. Knowing your speed not only helps you organize your day better, but helps you see if your efficiency is improving.

Afterword

When I was sixteen, my father and I took a car trip out to Vancouver Island. Even though my Mom and Dad owned and operated a large music store, he always took time off in the summer and did something special with me.

While in Vancouver, he stopped in at a store to visit with one of his many friends in the piano business. I took the opportunity to pop into the guitar shop next door.

At the time, I thought that I was the hottest sixteen-year-old guitarist in the country. I didn't really have any basis for that belief, but nevertheless, I still thought I was mighty good.

While I was looking for a suitable axe to pick up and wail on, a little boy, not more than nine or ten, walked in, picked up a Stratocaster, and played things I hadn't even imagined.

Totally disillusioned, I walked out, sat in the car and waited for my dad to return. Although I was feeling very depressed, I tried to put on a brave face for my dad when he returned.

"So, did you find a nice guitar to play?" he aske,d as he settled into his seat.

"Not really," I replied. "How was your friend?"

"He has a beautiful store!" he said, his face lighting up. "Great pianos, a great shop, everything a piano man could ask for."

It seemed as though perhaps my dad had just had a similar experience, and I sat in silence for a while thinking about what he had just said.

"Is it better than yours?" I asked.

Dad looked at me quizzically for a moment – a puzzled, almost sad expression on his face.

"Son," he finally answered, "nobody ever has anything better than what you have. The most anybody can have is something different. I have no idea what it took for him to get where he is, but I bet it wasn't a cakewalk."

I learned many things from my dad, much of it not about pianos. However, everything is related.

"Never envy anybody else," he told me. "Many people have it a lot worse."

Although I often see piano tuners that need a lot of improvement, I constantly meet tuners whose skills are much greater than mine. One of the best things about this career is that there is always room for improvement.

In a job where problem-solving, compromise, and patience are the key skills needed, you can never rest on your laurels and think you know it all. It just isn't possible.

Every day brings a new piano, and with it, a new challenge. Whether you're just starting to tune, or have been tuning for decades, I sincerely hope that this book has helped to kindle (or re-kindle) an interest and a passion for "The Art of Compromise".

James (Jamie) Musselwhite.

About the Author...

Jamie Musselwhite grew up among the sound of pianos and piano tuning. His father, Caleb Henry (Cal) Musselwhite, and his grandfather, Fredrick William, were both piano technicians, and today, he and his brother, John, carry on the family tradition.

For close to a half-century, Jamie has tuned, repaired and rebuilt pianos professionally, but his love of pianos stems from being a young boy literally learning at the knee of his father.

Jamie has tuned for orchestras, ballet and opera companies, and universities in Victoria, Calgary, Saskatoon, Winnipeg and Toronto, and for artists as diverse as Anton Kuerti, Victor Borge, The Pointer Sisters, Burton Cummings and Alice Cooper.

Although he was born and raised a prairie boy, Jamie now lives in Toronto, Canada.

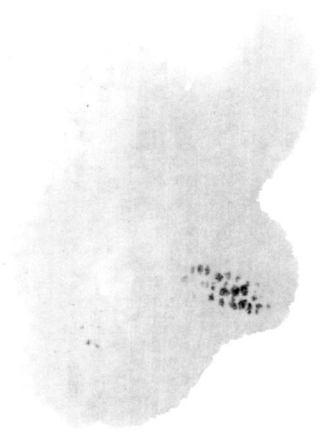

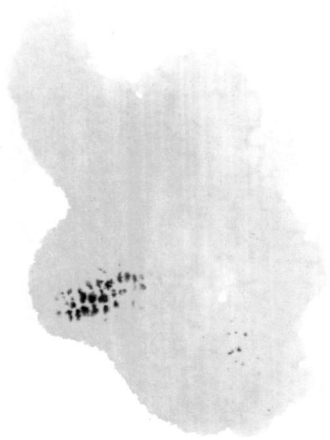